W9-BUE-663

small group MINISTRY
in the 21st century

the encyclopedia of practical ideas

Bible studies
spiritual growth
service projects

special events

Group

Loveland, Colorado

www.group.com

Group resources actually work!

This Group resource helps you focus on **"The 1 Thing™"**—a life-changing relationship with Jesus Christ. "The 1 Thing" incorporates our **R.E.A.L.** approach to ministry. It reinforces a growing friendship with Jesus, encourages long-term learning, and results in life transformation, because it's:

Relational
Learner-to-learner interaction enhances learning and builds Christian friendships.

Experiential
What learners experience through discussion and action sticks with them up to 9 times longer than what they simply hear or read.

Applicable
The aim of Christian education is to equip learners to be both hearers and doers of God's Word.

Learner-based
Learners understand and retain more when the learning process takes into consideration how they learn best.

Small Group Ministry in the 21st Century: The Encyclopedia of Practical Ideas!
Copyright © 2005 Group Publishing, Inc.

Visit our Web site: **www.group.com**

Credits
Editor: Brad Lewis
Creative Development Editor: Matt Lockhart
Chief Creative Officer: Joani Schultz
Copy Editor: Loma Huh
Book Designer and Art Director: Jenette McEntire
Assistant Art Director: Jean Bruns
Cover Art Director: Jeff A. Storm
Cover Designer: Ray Tollison
Illustrator: Gil Adams
Production Manager: Peggy Naylor

Unless otherwise noted, Scripture taken from the HOLY BIBLE, NEW INTERNATIONAL VERSION®. Copyright © 1973, 1978, 1984 by International Bible Society. Used by permission of Zondervan Publishing House. All rights reserved.

Small group ministry in the 21st century / [contributors, M. Scott Boren].--
1st American pbk. ed.
       p. cm.
ISBN 0-7644-2769-5 (pbk. : alk. paper)
1. Church group work. 2. Small Groups--Religious aspects--Christianity.
I. Boren, M. Scott.
BV652.2.S58 2004
253'.7--dc22
                           2004018866

10 9 8 7 6 5 4 3 2 1   14 13 12 11 10 09 08 07 06 05
Printed in the United States of America.

Table of Contents

Contributors

Many thanks to the following men and women—pastors, writers, and veteran small group leaders—who have provided the hundreds of ideas contained in this volume.

M. Scott Boren	James W. Miller
Kent Eilers	David B. Peterson
David P. Gallagher	Kristi Rector
Cheryl Gochnauer	Dean Ridings
Linda Holloway	Michael W. Sciarra
Brenda Jank	Steve Sonderman
Jeanette Gardner Littleton	Lee Warren
Mark Littleton	Ted Whaley
Matt Lockhart	

Special thanks to Brad Lewis, the compiling editor, and to Lyman Coleman, in general for his devotion, vision, inspiration, and heart for small groups; and specifically for writing the Introduction to this volume and his endorsement of it.

Using This Resource

Welcome to *Small Group Ministry in the 21st Century: The Encyclopedia of Practical Ideas!*

In this volume you will find eight sections with forty-nine lists, which contain over six hundred ideas for small group leaders. In addition to the Contents page, there is a page at the start of each section that outlines the content in that section.

This book is a collection of practical ideas. While you can read it from cover to cover, it is designed as a reference tool. In the Contents listing, look up the areas of small group ministry for which you need tips and ideas, and go from there. Within the various lists you will also find cross-reference notes that link you to related ideas.

You will see that several of the pages throughout this book have been noted as "OK to copy." (Look for the logo shown in the margin.) When using these pages, you may want to specifically put copies of them in the hands of your small group. If there are other pages with ideas you would like to copy for use with your immediate small group, you may do so. However, if the leader of another group or class wants copies of these ideas, that leader must purchase a copy of this book.

TO COPY

We pray that this tool will help you be an even more effective small group leader as you serve Christ by serving your group. May God bless you and your group!

Introduction

by Lyman Coleman

Four score and seven years ago, a man by the name of John Casteel wrote a book called *Spiritual Renewal Through Personal Groups*. In this book, he chronicled the stories of seven churches that dreamed of a new kind of church where people could really care for one another. I remember reading this book when I was a student in seminary and saying to myself, "If it can happen in seven churches, it can happen in every church in America."

The Three Pillars

Back in those days, there were three guarantees that held society together: (1) the extended family, (2) the guaranteed job, and (3) the secure neighborhood. Grandma lived next door. The job was for life, and the neighborhood church was around the corner. All of that has changed.

Today, grandparents come to see you at Christmas, Mom and Dad fight to keep their jobs, and the neighborhood is protected by security devices. We have two cars, three bedrooms, two baths, a boat, a bike, an entertainment center with surround sound, a vacation every year in the sun, and…we are running scared because we have no one to call on when things get tough at 3 a.m.

A Church in Dallas

I remember asking the leaders of a church in Dallas on a retreat to answer the question, "If you were going through a personal crisis and you needed four friends to drop everything and come to be with you to see you through this crisis, who would you call on?" One of the women said she would call on the sisters in her college sorority. A couple of the men said they would call on their army buddies. The pastor said that he would call on some men from his seminary days. A few admitted they had no one to call on. When it was all through (after two hours) I asked the group, "Did any of you think of calling on the other members of this group?" The silence was deafening.

I Stand by the Door

Today, the small group is accepted (even encouraged) in church circles. Some churches have completely restructured the way they "do church" around small care units. My challenge to small group leaders is to remember the roots that gave birth to this movement. I rejoice as I see the growth in the small group movement in the American church. But in all of this euphoria, I am concerned that we may have lost some of the passion that we had in the early days for people outside of the church.

One of the pioneers of the small group movement was an Episcopal priest by the name of Sam Shoemaker. He got his start in the Oxford Group movement as a student in Oxford, England. They lived by a set of rules that became known as the Oxford Group Rules. When Sam was ordained, they gave him the Episcopal Church in the garment district of New York City on Twenty-Third Street. Father Sam immediately claimed every person in his parish for God and explained to the prostitutes and pimps on the street that he was their priest: "Please call on me if ever I can be there for you."

After a few years, the Episcopal hierarchy moved Sam to the big church on Fourth Avenue called Calvary Episcopal. Father Sam immediately claimed everyone in this parish for God and started a mission around the corner for drunks, where a man by the name of Bill Wilson found help. Bill found that he could stay sober if he was helping another drunk to stay sober, but the Oxford Group Rules were a little complicated for drunks to understand, so Father Sam and Bill rewrote the rules and called them the Twelve Steps.

If Father Sam were alive today, I know what he would say to small group leaders who are starting a small group, and I would like to pass it along to you:

(An excerpt from Sam Shoemaker's poem "I Stand by the Door")

> I admire the people who go way in.
> But I wish they would not forget how it was
> Before they got in. Then they would be able to help
> The people who have not yet even found the door,
> Or the people who want to run away again from God.
> You can go in too deeply, and stay in too long,

And forget the people outside the door.
As for me, I shall take my old accustomed place,
Near enough to God to hear Him, and know He is there,
But not so far from people as not to hear them,
And remember they are there, too.
Where? Outside the door—
Thousands of them, millions of them.
But—more important for me—
One of them, two of them, ten of them,
Whose hands I am intended to put on the latch.
So I shall stand by the door and wait
For those who seek it.
"I had rather be a door-keeper..."
So I stand by the door.

So here is my challenge to you as a leader of a small group: Don't forget the door people, inside and outside the door of your church.

Here's to your ministry. Here's to what God is going to do through you as a minister of Jesus Christ.

FIRST STEPS
Ways to Get Your Group Going

SECTION 1: Table of Contents

First Steps—
Ways to Get Your Group Going

Congratulations! You've done something very admirable—you've made a wonderful commitment to serve God by leading a small group. Of course, you can't minister to empty chairs. The good news is that there are people who would love to learn about your small group and fill those chairs. So how do you let people know that there's a seat saved for each of them? And what do you do once you get people in those seats? This section will help you take the first steps as a leader to get your group started.

6 QUESTIONS TO HELP YOU PROMOTE YOUR GROUP

Answering the following questions about your group can help you do a bang-up job of promoting your small group.

1. Who's your audience?

The first key to effective communication is having a good picture of who your audience is. Who do you want to let know your group exists? Is your small group for couples, men only, women only, individuals of a certain age? Is your group service-oriented, or focused on issues? Perhaps your group is for seekers or new Christians, for people of all ages and stages, or for people who are mature in their faith. Looking at what kind of people your group is for will help you determine who your audience is.

Once you have a clear idea of the people you'd like to invite to your group, you're off to a good start for publicizing this opportunity.

2. What do you want them to do?

Next, think through what you'd like the people who learn of the opportunity to do. Certainly, you want them to investigate the possibility that this is an opportunity (among many) that's right for them. You want them to attend your small group, give it a go, and see if it's what they're looking for.

In light of this, whenever and wherever you have an opportunity to promote your group, make sure you reflect, as applicable, the following considerations:

- We're open to new members.

- You can drop in anytime; you're always welcome.

- If you sense the Lord leading you to become a member of our group, wonderful!

- Know that we won't pressure you into "signing on the dotted line."

- This might not merely be a group that God uses to work in you, but, because of how God has uniquely designed and gifted the body of Christ, it will most certainly be a group that God uses to work through you in the lives of others in the group as well.

- The "5 W's and H"—that is, anticipate the prospective participant's questions by thinking through the *who, what, when, where, why,* and *how* of your small group.

3. Why should they join your group?

Your promotional efforts will strike the bull's-eye of your target audience when you plan your promotion with the particular audience in mind and "go" to where they're located. In addition, potential group members will consider taking advantage of the opportunity when they hear that your group is addressing needs that hit home for them.

As people attempt to balance competing time demands, they often ask, "What's in it for me?" For example, some people have a desire to pray with others. What place will prayer have in your group? Are you planning to regularly set aside time to pray every meeting? Will the group sometimes spend the entire meeting in prayer? Others want extended times of praise and worship singing. Is your group going to have a concentrated time of praise and worship singing? And still others are primarily looking for ways to grow deep in the Lord, to focus on the "meat" rather than the "milk" of God's Word.

Is your group going to focus on in-depth Bible study, or is it a group designed to help people get to know each other or to introduce people to basic Christian principles?

Be clear in your promotion what your group *is*, and by so doing you'll also reflect what it *is not*.

Prospective members will consider getting involved in your group when they hear your first-person story of how God has used the group in your life, or when they hear the stories of others (especially if they know you and/or the other members of your group and have seen the effects of the group with their own eyes!). It's still true: The best form of advertising is word of mouth.

Finally, most people will consider trying out your group when they know that they're welcome, that they can "take it for a test-drive," and that attending one meeting doesn't constitute being an official member of the group just yet!

4. Where and how should you promote your group?

Of course, it's natural that you'll promote your group in your church, and a variety of ways exist to do this. Again, the most effective form of promotion is word of mouth. Make people you know aware of your small group.

- Tell others you meet at church.
- Encourage group members to tell people in their relational network.
- Let your pastoral staff know about your group and see if you can make an announcement from the pulpit—whether for small groups in general or your group in particular.

How else can you let prospective group members in your church know about your small group? Consider these communication opportunities:

- Brochure/listing of all small groups in the church
- Periodic small group "open house" meetings
- Staff a small group table in the church foyer
- Web site article
- Bulletin insert or announcement

- Strategically distributed fliers
- Print or electronic church newsletter

Beyond your church walls, you may want to promote your small group in the greater community where you live. Maybe you have a small group that simply meets regularly to read the Bible together. Such a group is ideal for non-Christians or nominal Christians in your neighborhood, but they don't know that it exists until you tell them. Some of your neighbors might love to know that you're reading the Bible and talking about whatever comes to mind in response to what you're reading—perhaps they've always wanted to read the Bible, but when they tried on their own, they simply didn't understand what they were reading.

So how do you get word out in your community?

- Go door to door.

- Create a flier and put it in a centrally located place (a community meeting room, a neighborhood bulletin board, and so forth).

- Develop relationships with your neighbors (host a neighborhood Christmas party, or have neighbors in for dinner, dessert, and/or a movie), and let them know in the natural course of conversation that you're hosting a group. If they're interested, they can give it a try once or twice without committing long-term.

5. What should we do if someone expresses an interest in joining the group?

Make it a priority to follow up with each person who expresses an interest in and/or attends your group. You can do this in person, by phone, or via e-mail. On behalf of the others in your group, let the interested person know

- We're glad you came.

- We're glad to answer any questions you may have.

- No pressure, but we'd like to have you visit again.

- If for any reason you're thinking this isn't the group for you, that's OK too! If you can briefly describe what it is you're looking for, perhaps we can connect you with another small group that may be a better fit.

6. Are you praying?

As you promote your group in your church and community, keep in mind the love that led Jesus to weep as he overlooked Jerusalem (Luke 19:41).

There are helpless, hopeless, and hurting people in your church and community who need to hear about Jesus and the needs you're helping meet in your small group. Pray that Jesus' heart is yours, and that this is reflected not only in how you serve as a small group leader but in every aspect of your promotional efforts as well. Pray that God will connect people in need with the opportunity that exists in your group.

Finally, don't think of promotion as a one-time event. As long as you have room to grow—and this should always be the case for small groups, with the goal of "birthing" a new group when yours becomes too large—consider promotion an ongoing process.

6 AGENDAS FOR SMALL GROUP MEETINGS

One of the best things you can do for members of your small group is to keep things on a solid schedule. Of course, you want to be open to God's leading during your meetings, and you don't want to be overly legalistic about schedules. Still, most of the time, it makes sense for group members to know when you'll start, what will happen during your meetings, and that you'll end on time.

Depending on the type of group you lead, here are some agendas or schedules your group can follow or adapt to fit your needs.

Bible-reading "seeker" group

You might be surprised how many unchurched people are interested in getting together weekly simply to read through the Bible. The group selects a meeting place, invites others (from school, work, the community, and so forth), pulls together copies of a reader-friendly Bible translation, and then participants gather to read for a certain amount of time. Afterward, the leader facilitates a short discussion.

Schedule: From 7:00 to 8:30 or 9:00 p.m.

7:00–7:15 p.m.	Touch base.
7:15–8:00 p.m.	Read a segment of Scripture: Individuals who desire to read aloud may take a portion of Scripture at a time, such as a certain number of verses or a chapter, and then rotate to the next reader. Individuals are invited to keep a notebook handy to write down questions or comments they may wish to discuss during the open discussion.
8:00–8:25 p.m.	Open discussion (led by facilitator).
8:25–8:30 p.m.	Closing prayer.
8:30–9:00 p.m.	Dessert/fellowship time (optional).

Women's tea time "seeker" group

A tea time small group might meet just once a month, such as the first Thursday of the month. The meeting rotates from home to home of group members and/or meets at local restaurants. Host responsibilities rotate among the regular participants, and the host selects the theme and spiritual emphasis of the gathering. This is a group where members can invite community or church acquaintances and friends.

Schedule: From 1:00 to 3:00 p.m.

1:00–1:30 p.m.	Gather, get to know new participants, "catch up" since last meeting.
1:30–2:30 p.m.	Tea and/or lunch or dessert, and socializing around the theme. In light of the selected theme, the host may invite members to bring along personal items, such as a favorite teacup or wedding pictures, for "show and tell."
2:30–2:50 p.m.	Spiritual emphasis: This isn't a time to preach or delve deeply into God's Word. It's a gentle message. The host might read a meaningful Bible passage, share an inspirational story, or read a short devotional.
2:50–3:00 p.m.	Brief closing prayer time.

CROSS REFERENCE:

"6 Ways Small Groups Can Meet the Needs of Women," Section 8, page 242

Men's accountability group

Saturday morning seems to be a good time for guys to get together, but the following agenda could also be adapted easily for a weekday gathering. In an accountability group, the leader builds an atmosphere of trust, and the group makes a commitment of confidentiality so all participants feel comfortable sharing what's going on in their lives. Men meet at a coffee shop, restaurant, or office and give one another permission to ask tough questions about wife, kids, relationships, job, and so forth.

Schedule: From 6:00 to 8:00 a.m.

6:00–6:30 a.m.	Socializing.
6:30–7:30 a.m.	Quick opening prayer followed by discussion. Here's an opportunity to go around the room or ask for volunteers to go one at a time (with everyone ultimately having a chance to share) as fellow group members ask tough questions of one another. Or you can go around the room and ask questions such as "What's the best thing presently going on in your life? What's the worst thing?"
7:30–8:00 a.m.	Prayer for one another based on what members of the group have shared.

CROSS REFERENCE:

"12 Principles for Men's Small Groups," Section 8, page 236

Outdoor adventure group

An outdoor adventure small group commits to getting together regularly, perhaps once a month, for support, encouragement, and exercise. Activities vary according to location, time of year, and fitness levels and needs. One month the group may take a hike, the next month a bicycle ride, and so forth.

Schedule: Varies depending on activity. Here's an example based on meeting from 7:30 to 10:30 a.m.

7:30–7:45 a.m.	Touch base with one another/get to know new participants.
7:45–8:00 a.m.	Warm-up exercises as the group leader details the day's activity.
8:00–10:00 a.m.	Outdoor activity.
10:00–10:30 a.m.	Snacks/debrief: The small group leader or another prearranged participant might share a personal story or inspirational word related to the activity, facilitate a brief discussion, and then close in prayer.

Midday video study group

Pull together a group of participants—at work, in your neighborhood, or friends from other activities—who can manage an extended lunchtime for a midday video study. You could use a video series featuring a speaker and a leader's guide that contains study questions. Or your group might choose to view segments of a popular movie. You can create your own movie discussion questions, check local Christian bookstores for whole books of movie discussions, or search online for similar studies.

Schedule: 12:00–2:00 p.m.

12:00–12:05 p.m.	Opening prayer.
12:05–12:30 p.m.	Potluck or brown-bag lunch and socializing.
12:30–1:00 p.m.	View segment of the movie or video study series.
1:00–1:30 p.m.	Discussion of video segment. Again, questions may be included if you use a prepackaged topical video series; or you can develop questions based on group members' needs and experiences.
1:30–2:00 p.m.	Praise reports/prayer requests/closing prayer.

Traditional weekly Bible study group

A traditional spiritual growth group puts the accent on the "teaching" time. Groups of six to twelve people get together weekly to study God's Word. The small group leader may take either a teacher or facilitator approach. This group may focus on the intense study of a particular book of the Bible, a topical Bible study series, or a spiritual growth book study.

Schedule: Bible study groups might meet early in the morning before work or school, or in the evenings on any given day throughout the week. Here's a sample evening schedule for 7:00 to 8:30 or 9:00 p.m.

7:00–7:10 p.m.	Welcome and check in with one another.
7:10–7:30 p.m.	Worship: an inspirational time of corporate singing—focusing on who God is, what he's done and is doing, and what he's promised to do—led by a group member with or without accompanying guitar, piano, or CD. This time prepares group members' hearts to receive God's Word.
7:30–8:15 p.m.	This is the Bible study and discussion time. As the leader, be sensitive to God's leading as you facilitate the discussion. Keep in mind that the goal of effective small group Bible study is not gaining knowledge for the sake of knowledge, but rather life change— applying biblical truth in our everyday lives.
8:15–8:30 p.m.	Praise reports/prayer requests/closing prayer.
8:30–9:00 p.m.	Optional snack or dessert/fellowship.

CROSS REFERENCE:
"14 Ideas for Small Group Worship Times," Section 5, page 145

6 SMALL GROUP CHILD-CARE SOLUTIONS

Before long, most groups face the challenging issue of what to do about child care. In fact, you may hear potential members say that they can't even visit your group because they can't find anyone to care for their children. The good news is that you can be proactive and help solve the problem before it starts. Try these ideas in your group.

1. Sink or swim

Perhaps the easiest approach is for group members to be responsible for making their own child-care arrangements. However, if you make child care a group concern, you give the group an early opportunity to practice the value of community.

2. On-site child care

If you meet in a home or other location that's conducive to this, group members can bring children along to your meetings, and parents can pay for on-site child care on a child-by-child basis.

Of course, it's wise to prescreen any potential child-care worker— paid or volunteer—who watches children as part of a church-sanctioned activity (even a home Bible study). Check with your church to see if it has a screening process in place that your group can use.

3. Older kids care for younger ones

If some small group members have older children who are mature enough to watch younger children, your group can pay these kids to watch or even to put on a lesson for the younger kids during the group's meeting.

4. Recruit from the church youth group

Check to see if the high school group at your church would be interested in providing child care as a youth group fundraiser. Again, be mindful that any young person who watches children should be certified, screened, and under adult supervision.

5. Piggyback with existing child care

Could your small group meet at church at a time when child care is already available? Just be careful not to take advantage of volunteers who provide this care. For example, you may need to adjust how long your group meets each week to fit the child-care schedule.

6. Group members rotate

If most or all of your group members have young children, give the members of the group the opportunity to serve each other by rotating the child-care responsibility among group members. Ideally, this would take place on-site where the group is meeting. This way there is no need for another stop to pick up kids, and after the meeting is over everyone—children included—can enjoy some informal fellowship time.

13 PRACTICAL WAYS TO MAKE EVERY MEETING COUNT

Often, the practical things you do to prepare for the meetings of your small group are just as important as making sure you're in the right place spiritually. Make the most of your small group meetings with these practical ideas.

1. Even though you can probably lead your study with minimal preparation time, take time to preview the lesson during the week. Highlight questions you feel are important for your group to spend time on, and make note of any supplies you might need.

2. Before your group is scheduled to meet, make sure the meeting environment is ready. Is the temperature comfortable?

Do you have enough chairs? Are the chairs arranged so that no one is outside the circle? How's the lighting? Do you have all the supplies you will need? What about refreshments? Is the bathroom presentable and is there toilet paper? Details like these are important components of a great meeting.

3. Prior to the start of your meeting, make an effort to personally welcome and greet each person as he or she arrives.

4. Have refreshments available at the start of a meeting. Build in ten to fifteen minutes of snack time before officially starting. This way, if people are running a few minutes late, they won't miss the beginning of the session.

5. Do what you can to avoid interruptions during the meeting time. If practical, don't answer the phone. Also, at the start of the lesson, ask people to turn off or down cell phones and pagers.

6. Always start on time. If you do this faithfully from the first meeting, you'll avoid the group arriving and starting later and later each week.

7. Don't hesitate to divide into small groups to discuss questions during your study or for prayer times. This encourages greater participation by everyone in the group and starts to develop leadership in others.

8. Encourage everyone to participate, but be careful not to put anyone on the spot. Let the group members know upfront that they can pass on questions they're not comfortable answering.

9. Keep your group on track. Encourage good discussion, but don't be timid about calling time on a given question and moving on. Part of your job is clock management. If the group decides to spend extra time on a given question or activity, consider skipping or spending less time on a later question or activity in order to stay on schedule.

10. Before dismissing the group, confirm the time and place of your next gathering. Also, make sure that whoever is responsible for refreshments at the next meeting is aware of his or her responsibility.

11. End on time. Regardless of where you are in the lesson, when the clock rolls around to the "advertised" ending time, call time and give group members the opportunity to leave if they need to. Then wrap up as quickly as you can. This communicates that you value and respect people's time.

12. Be prepared for people who want to hang out and talk after the meeting. If for any reason you (or the host) need people to leave by a certain time, be sure to make this clear during the meeting.

13. Thank people for coming, and let them know that you look forward to seeing them again at the next meeting.

8 DO'S AND DON'TS FOR YOUR FIRST MEETING

The launch of your small group is an exciting event. You're taking a diverse group of individuals and forming them into a community. The people come from different backgrounds and families, have different likes and dislikes, span a range of ages, and possess different spiritual maturities. Some will be skeptical, some shy. Chances are, someone will be a bit overbearing. Your goal is to create an atmosphere that allows people to blend comfortably and not feel threatened. You want to give hope for the future.

With all of that in mind, consider a few ground rules for how you'll lead the group's first meeting.

1. *Don't begin with preconceived expectations.*

It takes time for people to trust you and each other. So while you want to do the best job you can to lead and facilitate, avoid setting unrealistic expectations. Take what you get and build from there.

2. Don't allow people to feel pressured.

Give people the freedom to participate as they feel comfortable. Be careful not to put someone on the spot.

3. Don't ask people to read aloud until you know they are comfortable doing so.

Keep in mind that some people have reading disabilities. The last thing you want to do is embarrass someone.

4. Don't assume everyone will want to pray aloud.

Encourage individuals to pray if they want to, and then you can close. For many people it takes time before they feel comfortable praying in front of others.

CROSS REFERENCE:

"13 Approaches to Group Prayer," Section 1, page 48

5. Don't ask people to give spontaneous "testimonies."

In addition to some people being shy, others in your group may not be Christians or know what a testimony is! (In fact, it's best to avoid using church lingo.)

6. Do ask people to let you know if they feel uncomfortable praying or reading aloud.

It will be such a relief for people to be able to let you know that they don't like to read or pray in public. You can also let them know they can change their minds if they begin to feel more comfortable with other group members.

7. Do ask people ahead of time if they're willing to share their faith stories.

By lining up people ahead of time, you'll get a good sense of who feels comfortable sharing and who doesn't. This also gives people time to prepare what they want to say—and lessens the chance they'll ramble on and on.

8. Do ask for volunteers to read Scripture.

Simply asking, "Would someone like to read verses 28 and 29?" gives people a chance to read aloud if they want to. If no one volunteers after a few seconds, say "OK, I'll go ahead and read that passage."

3 FIRST MEETING FELLOWSHIP IDEAS

One of the goals of your first meeting is to help people get to know each other. The following ideas are low-key and nonthreatening but provide a good way to help people make an initial connection with other participants in the group.

1. Mixing game

The goal is to have four people seated together for about fifteen to twenty minutes and then move to another table to meet others. Set up card tables and number them. Choose or modify a card game or board game so that it can be played in fifteen-minute rounds. At the end of each round, have two people stay and two people move to the table with the next number. Keep the games simple and short—even modify the rules if need be to make them as simple as possible.

2. People bingo

On a piece of paper, create a five-by-five table—like a bingo card. In each square, list potential experiences that will be true of different individuals (such as "born in another state"; "married high school sweetheart"; "never used a cell phone"; "has a cat and a dog").

Copy and distribute the cards. Group members will then search for others who are a match for the various experiences. When someone finds a match, have that person initial the appropriate box. The catch is that group members need to have a different person for each box, and a person can only sign off one time for a given item.

For example, if Joe had Mary sign off on his card as the person who has a dog and cat, Mary cannot sign off for that same item on anyone else's card.

You can play this a couple of different ways: Play until someone gets five in a row (up, down, or diagonally), or you can play with the goal of seeing how many total squares people can find matches for in a set amount of time (such as three minutes).

3. Believe it or not

Have each group member write an amazing, unique, or unusual (but unknown) fact about him- or herself on an index card. Collect the cards, and then pass out paper with each group member's name listed next to a blank space. As you read each of the cards aloud, have group members use their lists to record their guesses about whom each fact belongs to. See who can correctly match the most facts with the names.

The value of this exercise is in the conversations that will arise as people ask for explanations of the things they discover about each other.

2 FIRST MEETING DEVOTIONAL IDEAS

Your first meeting can also include a simple Bible study or devotional component. Here are two ideas that even unchurched people will feel comfortable participating in.

1. The "one anothers"

Explore the "one anothers" in Scripture. Choose one or more of the following passages and read them through in the group. Discuss ways that people can live out these principles, as well as examples that you see in your families and in the cultures of people following or not following them.

- "Love one another"—John 13:34-35; Romans 13:8. See also John 15:12, 17 and 1 Thessalonians 4:9.
- "Accept one another"—Romans 15:7

CROSS REFERENCE:
"13 Ways to Live Out 'One Anothers,'" Section 4, page 115

  - "Serve one another in love"—Galatians 5:13
  - "Carry each other's burdens"—Galatians 6:2
  - "[Bear] with one another in love"—Ephesians 4:2

- "Be kind and compassionate to one another" —Ephesians 4:32
- "Encourage one another"—1 Thessalonians 5:11; Hebrews 3:13

2. Early church small groups

Acts 2:41-47 provides a look into the New Testament church and some of the very first small groups. Read the passage and ask your group to talk through the following questions.

- What were some of the things these early Christians did?
- How did this make the people feel?
- How did they demonstrate their love?
- What was the result?

10 EASY WARM-UPS

The purpose of a warm-up (some people call them icebreakers) is to open your small group meeting in a fun way that helps people connect to each other—and to the topic you're studying, if possible—in an interactive, nonthreatening, and relationship-building way. In general, allow about fifteen minutes for the group to work through the warm-up.

(These warm-ups have been taken and/or adapted from various Group Publishing HomeBuilders resources. For more information on these resources, see page 252.)

Busybodies

> **For this exercise, each group member needs**
> • a plastic knife
> • an item to balance on the knife, such as a coin, bean, button, or potato chip

Ask members of your group to stand in a circle with each person holding his or her plastic knife. Instruct group members to find an item to balance on the knife. Now tell them to continue holding the plastic knife, and to stand on one foot. Finally, doing all of the above, each group member should shake the hand of the person standing nearest to them.

Now discuss these questions:

• How would you compare this exercise to the life you live in today's culture?

• Do you feel like busyness is a problem in your life? Explain.

Sand Castles

> **For this warm-up you'll need the following items:**
> - a rock about the size of a softball
> - two or three cups of sand
> - a pitcher of water
> - a large pan, such as a 9x13 cake pan

Put the sand in the pan, and then pour a little water onto it—just enough to make the sand damp so it can be molded into shapes. Ask one or two group members to form a small sand castle on one side of the pan. When they're finished, place the rock on the other side of the pan.

Read Matthew 7:24-27. Now have someone pour the pitcher of water over the sand castle and the rock, and discuss these questions:

- What can we learn from this exercise? Write down your observations, then share them with the group.

- Why is a spiritual foundation like the one described in Matthew 7:24-27 necessary in our lives?

Introductions

Take a few minutes to introduce yourself to someone in your group that you don't know very well (preferably man to man and woman to woman). Find out each other's names, names of each other's spouses, names and ages of each other's children, and one other fact. After everyone has had a chance to visit, take turns introducing each other to the group.

Then discuss these questions:

• What do you find exciting and fun about getting to know someone?

• What aspects are intimidating or difficult?

• In what ways is introducing someone to others like or unlike introducing someone to Christ?

Back to Nature

Choose one of the following questions to answer, and share with the group.

- What outdoor activities do you enjoy doing?

- If you're married, what's one thing you've learned about your spouse by spending time together in the great outdoors that you didn't know when you first were married?

- When have you seen or experienced evidence of God in nature?

Superheroes

Form two groups. Have one group talk about the way the characters below are like God, and ask the other group to discuss how they are unlike God.

- Greek and Roman gods and goddesses
- Superheroes from movies, TV shows, and comic books
- Actors who have portrayed God or Jesus in movies and on TV

Ask each subgroup to report on its discussions, and then have the whole group discuss the questions below.

- What are some things that many people seem to believe about God but that aren't necessarily supported by Scripture?

- What do you think are the primary sources of information about God for most people?

Descriptions

Select one or two people from the list of names below and list a few words that you think best describe the people you chose.

- Albert Einstein
- Oprah Winfrey
- Martha Stewart
- Martin Luther King Jr.
- Tom Hanks
- Tiger Woods
- Jackie Chan

- Helen Keller
- Billy Graham
- Apostle Paul
- Queen Esther
- Hudson Taylor
- Jennifer Lopez

Share who you selected and what words you used to describe that person with the group.

Then discuss these questions:

- If you asked a child to describe God, what words do you think he or she would use?

- What are three or four words you'd use to describe God?

Just Like Mom or Dad

Select one or two of the following questions to respond to:

• As an adult, what are the most apparent ways you're like your mom or your dad?

• When you were growing up, who did your parents' friends say you took after—your mom or your dad?

• What kinds of things have you found that you can learn about a child's parents by observing the child?

• What's one way that knowing Jesus helps you better understand and know God?

Media Log

Think back to yesterday. How much time did you spend reading, watching, or listening to various types of entertainment or news media? Take a guess and fill in the time on the blanks below.

Music and radio: _____

TV/Movies: _____

Internet: _____

Newspapers/Magazines: _____

Books:_____

Video Games:_____

Other: _____

TOTAL: _____

Now answer these questions:

• What was your total?

• What do you see as good or bad about the variety of media you use on a given day?

• How do you think the amount of media you consumed yesterday compares with the amount of time you spent with God yesterday (in prayer, reading Scripture, and so forth)?

Following Instructions

Choose one or two of the following questions to answer, and share with your small group:

- What's something that one of your parents taught you to do well?

- If you're married, who's better at following instructions or directions—you or your spouse? Explain.

- When was a time you were glad you followed instructions?

- Can you remember a time when you didn't follow the directions? What happened?

- What's one biblical instruction you follow for guidance in living your life?

Reflections

Pair off members of the group, and have partners stand facing each other. One person in each pair can make any motions or facial expressions he or she wants to, and the other person must move as if a mirror image. After about a minute, have the partners switch roles. After another minute, everyone can sit down, and your group can discuss these questions:

• What was it like trying to follow your partner's actions?

• What was most important in order to follow successfully?

• In what ways is this exercise like trying to follow Jesus?

5 MEANINGFUL WRAP-UPS

The idea of a wrap-up is to close your small group meeting in an appropriate and meaningful way. A wrap-up helps reinforce the point of the meeting or study. Your group's wrap-up shouldn't take the place of prayer time, so allow about fifteen minutes for the wrap-up before your group's closing prayer.

(These wrap-ups have been taken and/or adapted from various Group Publishing HomeBuilders resources. For more information on these resources, see page 252.)

5 MEANINGFUL WRAP-UPS: Idea 1

Relationship Builders

Divide your small group into two or three subgroups and brainstorm lists of simple, low-cost, relationship-building activities your group could do together. Different subgroups could focus on different kinds of activities—pure fun, low-key, outreach-oriented, and so forth.

After compiling your lists, review them with the larger group and select one or two activities your group can do together in the next three months. If possible, ask for a volunteer to head up each activity, and ask that person to report progress to the group in two weeks.

Spiritual Journey

Read the following descriptions of points where various individuals might be on their spiritual journeys:

- Someone who has never taken time to seriously consider the truth of Scripture and the claims of Christ.
- Someone who is seeking truth, but hasn't come to a decision about whether or not to commit his life to Christ.
- Someone who has always thought she was a Christian but, when she took a closer look, realized she didn't have a personal relationship with Christ.
- Someone who has committed his life to Christ, but has always struggled with kind of a roller coaster faith—he goes through times of walking closely with Christ and other times of spiritual dryness.
- Someone who has made a personal commitment to Christ, and while she realizes she's still a sinner, she tries to walk consistently in trust and obedience to God.

Now read the following questions and record your responses. Relate your answers to the group, but only if you feel comfortable sharing.

- On your spiritual journey, where would you say you are?

- Do any of the above descriptions describe you? Or would you state them in a different way?

- In what ways does participating in this small group affect your view of God and your need for starting or deepening a relationship with him?

Seeing God

We sometimes forget that we can see God in so many places. As you think of a friend you'd like to see begin or strengthen a relationship with Christ, imagine how you could point out God in the following locations:

- at the beach

- out in the country, looking up at the stars on a clear night

- in a garden

- traveling together on a jet, looking out the window from thirty thousand feet

- at a local mall or shopping district

- on a mountain hike or bike ride

Now consider these questions:

- What different things could you point to at each location to help your friend understand more about knowing God?

- What is a nearby place you could invite your friend to go to "see" God?

Uniquely God

Spend some time as a group listing words that describe God's qualities, character, or attributes (for example, *holy, pure, righteous, loving, forgiving, merciful,* and so forth).

On your own, choose seven of those words that you'd like to explore more fully. Make a list, and assign one quality to each day of the week (for example, Monday: faithful; Tuesday: full of grace; and so on).

Sunday: _____

Monday: _____

Tuesday:_____

Wednesday: _____

Thursday: _____

Friday: _____

Saturday: _____

As a group, discuss easy and everyday ways you can learn more about these characteristics of God. Work on your list throughout the week, and be prepared to report next week—not on the facts you've learned, but on how your study into God's attributes changed how you view him and his relationship to you.

Power of Prayer

> *For this wrap-up, everyone will need an index card or piece of paper and something to write with.*

One of the most powerful things your small group can do for each other is pray. Prayer is a conversation with the Creator. God wants you to make your needs and burdens known to him in prayer.

Ask each member of your group to take a few minutes and silently reflect on his or her own life. Have each one think about needs, issues, or concerns.

If group members are comfortable doing so, have them write their names and the one thing that they'd like to have prayer for on index cards or pieces of paper, and put these requests in a bowl or hat. Take turns drawing requests until they all are distributed. If you draw your own, simply take a different one.

Spend some time in silent prayer, with each member of the group praying for the person and/or request listed on the drawn cards. Take the cards with you, and commit to keeping them someplace where they'll be kept in confidence, but where each of you will be reminded to pray regularly.

13 APPROACHES TO GROUP PRAYER

As you lead your group, the concept of modeling prayer is very important, especially if your group is meeting for the first time. One of the ways adults who are in an ongoing group can experience prayer is by the leader introducing different ways to pray over the course of the study. Use these ideas to get you started.

1. Leader prayer

For a first meeting where people may not know each other well, take prayer requests and then, as the leader, offer a closing prayer. To solicit prayer requests, ask the question, "How can our group pray for you this week?"

2. Volunteer prayer

You can learn who is comfortable praying aloud by asking for volunteers. In your second meeting, ask, "Who would like to close in prayer for us tonight?" Take prayer requests and have your volunteers pray.

3. Group prayers

Divide the larger group into pairs or groups of three or four. The people in these smaller groups can focus on praying for each other.

4. Sentence prayers

Another way to pray in a group is to have everyone complete short, simple sentence prayers. For example, ask everyone to complete one of the following sentences: "Lord, I want to thank you for…" or "Lord, I want to pray for…"

5. Silent prayer

Don't overlook the power of silent prayer. There's something moving about a room full of individuals all pouring out their hearts to God at the same time.

6. Assisted silent prayer

Read each prayer request aloud and pause briefly (for ten seconds or so) after each one to allow the group to pray before moving on to the next item.

7. Prayer circle

Form a circle with hands joined, and ask each person to take a turn praying. Make it clear that silent prayer is an option. A person who prays silently can squeeze the hand of the next person to indicate that he or she has finished praying.

8. Pray Scripture

Pray the Lord's Prayer or read a psalm. This can be done together or by breaking up the passage into parts. This is a form of scripted prayer that will make praying aloud easier for some.

9. Open prayer

Anyone can offer up a prayer or prayers. When doing this, it can be helpful to designate a person to open and a person to close the prayer time. Don't rush and don't be put off by some short periods of silence.

10. Domino prayer

Ask everyone to "Pray for the person to your right or left—silently or aloud." If someone chooses to pray silently, ask him or her to say "Amen" at the end of the prayer to indicate that he or she has finished praying.

11. Musical prayer

Sing a common chorus or hymn, such as the Doxology.

12. Planned prayer

Read a prayer from a book of prayers.

13. Ending prayer

Make a final session or meeting's prayer time special by asking the group to stand together in a circle. Each group member can take a turn standing or, if comfortable, kneeling in the center of the group as the group prays specifically for him or her.

40 QUESTIONS TO HELP YOU STAY SPIRITUALLY FOCUSED

God has given you the opportunity and privilege of serving him as you serve as the leader of a small group. In so doing, you follow in the path of Jesus himself, who maintained different levels of relationships in his earthly ministry. In your service as a small group leader who follows in the Master's footsteps, keep in mind that your standard must be his standard, one well reflected in the Apostle Paul's words: "Whatever you do, work at it with all your heart, as working for the Lord, not for men" (Colossians 3:23).

Use the following questions to prepare your own heart spiritually and to help you focus on the essentials as you lead your small group.

1. Before God, how am I doing personally?

2. Am I praying for myself?

3. How's my walk with God? Am I up to date with him?

4. Does Christ live in me?

5. Is he giving me victory?

6. Do I know that God's call and hand are upon me to serve him as a small group leader?

7. Am I personally prepared to lead?

8. Does my life, in increasing measure, reflect the characteristics of leaders based on 1 Timothy 3:1-7 and Titus 1:5-9?

9. Is there a need, for any reason, to "take myself out of the game" so I can get right with God?

10. Am I prayerfully considering the lesson, asking God to lead me through it in light of what he knows about each member of the group and their needs?

11. To what extent am I seeking to understand members' needs and adapting the lesson to address their needs?

12. Do I know where group members are in their faith, and is there a particular book study or series that God can use in their lives?

13. Does my preparation reflect that I am committed to looking at what the Bible says, what it means, and what it means to each of us?

14. Am I preparing in such a way that members will be able to talk, mull over the Bible, and move toward personal application?

15. Am I developing a support team—an apprentice leader, a host, a mentor/coach, or am I attempting to be a "lone ranger leader"?

16. Am I creating an environment where the "one another/each other" verses of the Bible can be lived out?

17. Are group members demonstrating in word and deed a commitment to each other—exhorting, encouraging, and praying for each other?

18. Are group members looking at God's Word (rather than a myriad of other sources of "understanding this world") and applying it to their lives?

19. Am I preaching or facilitating a discussion? As I guide the group through the lesson, is it a conversation? Do I give everyone the opportunity to speak?

20. Am I comfortable with silence as people mull over the personal implications of God's Word?

21. Am I more apt to be the "Bible answer person" or to ask, "What's the group's take on this"?

22. Do our group's studies move toward application? Am I asking, "In light of this lesson, what do you think God is trying to teach you?"

23. Am I teaching tradition or biases, or are we comparing Scripture with Scripture to get the fullest, most accurate meaning from a verse or passage?

24. Am I being sensitive to the Holy Spirit's leading?

25. Is one person dominating the discussion?

26. Do members have an opportunity to talk honestly, without "masks," about what's going on—their joys and struggles, hopes and fears, the best and worst moments of the week—especially in light of biblical truth and in time set aside for prayer?

27. Are group members sharing distant or surface prayer requests, or are the prayer needs personal and deep?

28. Am I sensitive enough to the Spirit's lead that I know when to scrap the lesson and devote the entire time to prayer?

29. Are we as a group keeping a record of how God answers prayer, and are we occasionally reviewing together how God is answering the group's prayers?

30. Are members talking about praise reports as well, sharing with fellow members what God has done and is doing?

31. Is there a sense of authentic worship from start to finish?

32. After each meeting, do I ponder what really hit home with group members in terms of the lesson?

33. How can I help each group member grow toward greater Christlikeness and biblical obedience?

34. Did each member of the group have a chance to share concerns and requests?

35. Is God meeting me at my point of need? Did I learn something new, relevant, and applicable right along with the group?

36. Is my small group keeping faith with its covenant—for example, not merely "inward focused" (helping members grow deeply in Christ) but "outward focused" (open to unchurched family members, friends, and neighbors)?

37. Am I regularly praying for each member of my group and the needs each brought up during the prayer time?

38. Am I reflecting God's love to each member of the group between meetings?

39. Am I calling, e-mailing, putting a card of encouragement in the mail, or touching base in person with each member regularly?

40. To what extent am I demonstrating a commitment to helping members find meaningful ministry not only inside but also outside the group?

FINE ART
Ways to Keep Your Group Going Strong

Fine Art—
Ways to Keep Your Group Going Strong

You've made it past your initial meetings, and your group is starting to gel. Now that you've got a solid core group of people meeting together, it's time to pull them together to decide how you'll live as a community of people growing closer to each other and to God.

12 WAYS TO DECIDE WHAT YOUR GROUP WILL STUDY

There are many wonderful options available for small group Bible studies. In addition to dedicated Bible studies, many best-selling books come with study guides included or available separately. Some guides go beyond learning the subject, and teach the students how to study Scriptures on their own. With so many options, your group's biggest challenge may be deciding what *not* to study. Use these principles to help guide your decision making.

CROSS REFERENCE:
"Appendix: Group Publishing's Small Group Resources," pages 252-253

1. Pray

Pray first! Don't begin the process of choosing a study until you first take it before God. Choosing a study is an important decision. It will set the direction of your group for several months. You're not just learning facts; you're studying the true and living Word of God. Lives will be changed. Old habits will be replaced. Relationship will be restored. Years from now, members of your group will remember the study with fondness. Remember, pray first!

2. Remember the purpose of your group

Every small group is different. As your group chooses a study, keep the purpose of the group in mind. Is the purpose evangelism? Then consider an apologetic type study. Is the purpose to find victory over addictions? Then check recommended books and studies listed in literature or on Web sites of ministries targeting addictions. If your group is part of a church's small group ministry, you'll also want to stay faithful to the objectives of the whole ministry and follow direction given by the ministry's leadership.

3. Evaluate the maturity of your group

Bible studies vary from simple to complicated. You want to see growth in the lives of the group members, so what you study needs to be challenging. You also want the Bible studies to be within everyone's grasp, yet you don't want anyone to be bored. Your group might agree to vary the difficulty of studies by starting with a simple study and then following up with a more challenging study. If one or two group members find a particular study too difficult, encourage the group to keep them engaged and not become discouraged. You may need to privately remind more mature group members to share your excitement in seeing growth in the lives of those younger in their faith.

4. Evaluate any special circumstances of group members

Are any members of your group going through life circumstances that could give deeper meaning to a particular study? For example, a study on heaven can be especially meaningful when someone has experienced a death in the family. Illness or other difficult times can provide an enriching connection for a study on prayer, the life of Job, God's sovereignty, or staying faithful.

CROSS REFERENCE:

"5 Ready-to-Go Special Occasion Bible Studies," Section 6, page 156

5. Keep the "seasons of life" of group members in mind

Each person is in some season of life—single, married, married with children, empty nest, retired. Consider a study that focuses on the needs unique to a particular season of life being experienced by some of your group members. For example, a study on the family can be valuable for everyone—those who've already raised their children can add wonderful perspective to this kind of study. Similarly, learning about aging is valuable to younger couples with aging parents.

6. Emphasize reaching out

If your small group was formed with evangelism in mind, choose a study that's attractive and that honestly addresses the questions that group members are asking. Resist the urge to use simplistic, answer-it-all studies—these can turn away the very people you're trying to draw in. Even if your group isn't primarily an evangelistic group, you may still have non-Christians attending. Be careful not to choose a study that causes them to feel like targets. Simply choose a more general study, and allow God to work in their hearts as they participate in the discussion with others.

7. Study spiritual disciplines

In the rotation of your studies, include a study of spiritual disciplines. These challenging subjects—such as prayer, Scripture reading, fasting, or Scripture memorization—will help everyone in your group grow spiritually. Take care to emphasize that spiritual disciplines are tools for growth, not measures of growth.

8. Agree to move beyond Bible knowledge

Studying a book of the Bible together can be a wonderful experience. But always keep in mind that the goal is not just to know more about the Bible. The goal is for the Bible to lead people to know Christ or know him better. Jesus said, "You diligently study the Scriptures because you think that by them you possess eternal life. These are the Scriptures that testify about me" (John 5:39).

9. Study Christian living skills

Choose a study that helps your group develop in a specific area of the Christian life. For example, study evangelism to learn how to evangelize. Study methods of Bible study. Work together to find each individual's spiritual gifts. Survey your group to find out the areas of their lives where they'd like to see growth.

10. Study practical living skills from a biblical perspective

The Bible has a lot to say about how we should live each day as we walk with God. From relationships to money to character and values, Scripture is full of guidelines about integrating our faith with everyday life. For example, your group might examine the following topics:

- Finances. There are thousands of verses in the Bible related to money.
- Parenting. "Children are a gift of the Lord" (Psalm 127:3, New American Standard Bible), but they're a gift that seems to come without the instruction manual.
- Marriage. Once we get married, how do we spend the rest of our lives learning how to live together?

11. Tackle contemporary issues

What are the latest headlines? Consider studies that help group members think wisely about issues that are in the media every day. Of course, studying a subject like genetics, gender roles, or origin of life can also be risky or divisive. Don't necessarily avoid these topics; just choose study material wisely.

12. Study relationship building

One of the best ways to for your group to learn how to be a community is to study the "one anothers" of Scripture, encouraging each other to live out these important principles. Remember, you're a group of "one anothers."

CROSS REFERENCE:
"13 Ways to Live Out 'One Anothers,'" Section 4, page 115

4 GUIDELINES FOR DEVELOPING A GROUP COVENANT

Every small group needs guidelines to function effectively. Your small group's covenant is a formal agreement that lays out the parameters of the small group so it doesn't spin out of control, fall apart, or lose its way. God used covenants with his people and considers this form of agreement important. A covenant is binding on all parties—but only as long as parties choose to be bound. Your small group's covenant helps hold members accountable to each other. Some groups, such as Bible study groups, prayer groups, or ministry training groups, prefer a written covenant. For other groups, something more informal might be in order. Use these ideas to help your group create its covenant.

1. Be a facilitator, not a dictator

As your small group is forming and putting together a covenant, you'll have more "buy-in" if you act as a facilitator while members generate ideas. A top-down list of rules simply isn't as effective as an agreement that the group as a whole creates.

2. Record all ideas from group members

Ask members of your group if they agree that drawing up an agreement for the small group would be beneficial. Discuss how having a covenant would be better than not having one. Ask if anyone has been in a small group previously, if those groups had covenants or ground rules, and what items were included. This can help initiate brainstorming about what your group's covenant should include. Stimulate the discussion, if necessary, by suggesting items as fundamental as time and place, and qualities such as being on time.

3. Divide and conquer

You can involve more people and move almost twice as fast if you split your group into two. One subgroup can work on the meeting details of your small group (time and place). The other group can focus on valued qualities (being on time, confidentiality). Facilitate the activity by writing ideas generated by each group on paper or a whiteboard. The group as a whole can then determine which items will be included in the covenant.

4. Ask the group to prepare in advance

Encourage group members to come to the meeting with a written list of ideas they believe should be incorporated in the group's agreement. Suggest that individuals leave their names off their lists. Write these items on paper or a whiteboard, and decide as a group which items will be included in your covenant.

13 ITEMS TO CONSIDER INCLUDING IN A GROUP COVENANT

Some items belong in almost every small group's covenant. While members of the group will probably suggest these items, if no one does, you can suggest those that appear to be appropriate for your group to consider.

Once you've agreed on what your covenant will include, draw up a formal covenant like a contract. Group members can sign and date the covenant, and you can make a copy for each individual. Periodically re-examine your covenant, particularly if the dynamics or purpose of your group changes.

1. Meeting time and location

This statement should include times the meeting will begin and end, the day of the week when your group will meet, the group's meeting place(s), and how often the group will meet.

2. Policy for dealing with exceptions to regular meeting time

What will your group do during severe weather, holidays, or an all-church function? Who will make calls or send e-mails to group members if necessary? Is your group large enough to set up a "phone tree"?

3. The purpose of your group

Is your group primarily a Bible study group? a fellowship group? a book study group? a craft group? What's the purpose of the activity? Is it to learn more about faith? Is it for young married couples to develop relationships with other young married couples? If you don't have a clear purpose, the group can easily veer off course. Listing your group's purpose in its covenant will help keep the group on track.

4. Commitment to starting and ending on time

This allows members to make your small group's meetings a priority and to plan their schedules around the meeting. If you consistently wait for people who are running late, you run the risk of giving others "permission" to be late, too. If your group's meeting consistently runs longer than you agree to, some members may stop participating, especially if they're dealing with a job or babysitters.

5. Commitment to arriving and leaving on time

This shows respect for the other individuals in the group, especially the hosts. It honors their time as important.

6. Attendance accountability

Agree that group members will contact you (the leader) if they can't attend a meeting. This lets you know how many members of the group to expect. If you face an unusual case of many absent members, you can even decide to cancel the meeting. This honors your time.

7. Commitment to confidentiality

Group members should be able to bring up issues or concerns and express their opinions without fearing that anyone outside the group will hear them. This helps foster trust and bonding within the group. What is said in the group should stay in the group. The exception to this is if someone threatens harm to others or themselves. If this should occur, take it seriously and seek immediate intervention and help.

8. Commitment to do "homework"

If your group has reading or study to do outside of the meeting time, members agree to complete it before the next meeting. The goal is enabling people to effectively share in group discussion because they're "on the same page" as the rest of the group.

9. Agreeing to participate in group discussions

Some shy members won't talk at all. Urge all participants to share, but don't embarrass those who can't think of anything to add at a particular point in the discussion.

10. Agreeing to take turns answering questions or talking in discussions

One or more members may monopolize your discussions if you don't agree to give each other time to speak. Occasionally, as the leader, you might need to give a gentle reminder. Say something like, "What do others think about what [person's name] is saying?" or "Do others have thoughts about that topic?" Using the word *others* is a good clue to the person dominating the conversation that it's time to be quiet for a while. Another way to build in maximum participation is to agree upfront that your group will regularly utilize smaller subgroups for discussion when appropriate.

11. Agreeing to attend meetings regularly, as well as scheduled social activities

For members of the group to form relationships, they need to be as faithful in attendance as they possibly can. Those who attend infrequently are more likely to feel like outsiders as the group grows together over time.

12. Commitment to pray for one another

Praying together can take many forms—prayer request lists, praying as God leads during corporate prayer times, or praying for each other between meetings.

CROSS REFERENCE: "13 Approaches to Group Prayer," Section 1, page 48; and "6 Ways to Make Group Prayer More Meaningful," Section 5, page 137

13. Agreeing on how to deal with conflict

Will disagreements be handled in the group or outside the group? Do you agree to disagree, but not to get hostile or angry with each other? Individuals with conflicting views should each make their point and then move on with the meeting. There are several applicable Bible passages related to conflict that you might want to reference within your covenant. Here are a few: Leviticus 19:18; Matthew 7:5, 12; 18:15-17; Ephesians 4:2-3, 25, 29, 32; Philippians 2:3-4.

7 BASIC WAYS TO DEAL WITH PROBLEMS IN YOUR GROUP

While your covenant will cover the general guidelines your group will follow to get along as a community, chances are good that it won't cover everything. Because your group is made up of human beings, you can't avoid problems. In fact, you don't want to avoid them. Problems give God an opportunity to deal with issues that keep your group from growing and moving on. They reveal the hidden issues of people's hearts that limit them and keep them bound up, without spiritual freedom.

Good leaders know how to deal with problems. You must learn to keep your eyes open for problems. Satan will seek to exploit disagreements and conflicts for his gain, but the Lord desires to deal with hearts and use problems to sharpen his people: "As iron sharpens iron, so one man sharpens another" (Proverbs 27:17). Use the following ways to deal with problems that arise in your group.

1. Pray

When you recognize a problem, your natural instinct is to react, to take action. You think, "I need to confront him," or "I need to tell her what to do." You might come to these conclusions because you took the same approach in the past and it worked. Don't depend on past experience. God wants you to seek him for the other person and allow him room to work. You might sense that God wants you to act. But you might also realize that you need to wait.

2. Look to Scripture

When it comes to dealing with problems in your group, search the Scriptures to see what God's Word has to say about the situation. For example, in regard to interpersonal conflict that might arise in a group, there are numerous Bible passages that provide a biblical basis for conflict resolution. (See point 13, "Agreeing on how to deal with conflict," on page 64.)

3. Develop a core

If you feel the pressure to deal with problems yourself, it might be a sign that you've taken all of the group's leadership on your own shoulders. A wiser approach is to invite two or three group members to work with you. These core members can help you pray for the group, provide feedback, and even deal with some of the administrative issues of leading a group.

CROSS REFERENCE:

"7 Roles to Get Group Members More Involved," Section 2, page 69

4. Identify an apprentice or intern

Pray that God will raise up a future leader you can mentor into a leadership role. This person will be a part of the group core, but he or she would take on the additional responsibility of helping you lead meetings and care for group members. This means that you always have support from at least one person as you deal with problems.

5. Take charge

Failing to do what you need to do—perhaps because you fear offending the source of the problem—is one of the worst things you can do. When you attain a clear sense of God's direction, you should do one thing: Obey. You also may face situations that require immediate action, such as when someone speaks against the leadership of the church, tries to spread false doctrine, or tries to give a group member bad advice. In these kinds of situations, people can get hurt, so you must act. Be the leader you are.

6. Talk with your pastor or small groups coach

Some problems you encounter will be beyond your ability or experience to address. It's a sign of maturity when you realize that you don't know what to do. Talk with the person who oversees you and your group.

7. Refer

If someone shares a chronic or potentially harmful problem— such as a troubled marriage, chronic depression, suicidal thoughts, sexual sins, or abuse—refer that group member to a pastor. Even better, go along to set up an appointment with the pastor and tell the group member that you can accompany him or her to the meeting if desired.

7 SPECIFIC PROBLEMS AND WAYS TO DEAL WITH THEM

1. The uncontrollable talker

- Ask questions this way: "In two or three sentences, how would you describe…"

- Ask specific people to answer your questions. This gives other people permission to contribute.

- Sit next to the talker. Eye contact is a permission-giving signal. When you sit next to someone, eye contact is very difficult.

- Interrupt. Even talkers have to breathe. Wait for a deep breath, jump in, and redirect the question to the rest of the group. Say, "That's a good point. Sally, how do you see this passage applying to your life?"

- Talk with the person privately. Ask him or her to help you get others involved, using the talker's boldness to your advantage.

- Develop a "stop" signal. In your private conversation, come up with a signal—like pulling your ear—so that the talker will recognize when he or she goes too far.

2. The rabbit-chasing group

- Interrupt someone who seems to be changing the subject from the main point of the lesson by reminding the whole group of the goal. Then redirect the question to someone else.

- Depend on your intern or apprentice. This person can support you during the meeting by bringing the group back to the main point.

- State the goal of the discussion upfront. If your group has problems with staying on track, this may be a crucial strategy.

- Pray. If someone shares a personal need during the discussion and you feel that it's inappropriate at that point in your lesson, say something like, "Thank you for sharing. May I pray for you right now?" Pray briefly and then get back on track.

3. A person with chronic needs

- Pray for the person after the meeting is over. This is especially important if this person shares his or her needs every week.
- Spend time together outside the group meeting.
- Ask another group member to spend some time with that person.
- Ask the help of a pastor or a coach.

4. A disruptive or argumentative visitor

- Explain the purpose of your group. This is especially important if the visitor is from another church and has a lot of small group experience. He or she may want to force a different agenda on the group, and you must make it clear that you won't let this happen.
- Direct questions to specific people so that the disruptive visitor doesn't have permission to take over.
- Keep the conversation going. Silence gives this person an open door to make his or her point.
- Interrupt. This is crucial when someone is giving harmful advice to other group members or saying something that's biblically unsound.

5. Group member conflict

- Help people understand that conflict is a natural part of relating to others. Groups that never experience conflict are failing to honestly relate to one another. If group members are growing in relationships, they're bound to have misunderstandings and hurt feelings.
- Mediate. Help people talk through their differences and misunderstandings.
- Practice forgiveness. You'll experience conflict yourself. You must model a healthy conflict by forgiving anyone who hurts you.

6. A stagnant group

- Invite new people. Challenge members to invite new people.
- Meet at a different time or place.
- Go on a daylong retreat and ask God for a vision for your group. If you don't have a vision, it will be almost impossible for the group to change.
- Take a break from the "usual" and do something different and fun.

CROSS REFERENCE:

"18 Ideas for Places to Meet," Section 3, page 86

"2 One-Day Retreats for Small Groups," Section 6, page 171

"22 Fun Small Group Activities," Section 3, page 89

7. An enormous group

- Identify a future leader and mentor that person. Without another leader, your group will be stuck. It will never multiply no matter how big it gets.
- Prepare the group for "multiplication." Explain to your group that multiplication is a future probability. Do this two or three months before you actually "birth" or start a new group.

CROSS REFERENCE:

"4 Best Endings for Small Groups," Section 2, page 78

- Break your group into smaller groups to discuss the lesson.

7 ROLES TO GET GROUP MEMBERS MORE INVOLVED

One way to solve problems and increase how connected people in your group feel to each other is by giving members an area of ministry that they can own. Not everyone in your group will want to take on a responsibility, but others will welcome the opportunity. As you think of ways to encourage positive involvement in the life of the group, keep these ministry positions in mind.

1. Prayer ministry coordinator

Recruit someone who is passionate about prayer to be the keeper of the prayer list, as well as the spark plug for letting your group know about urgent prayer needs that arise between group meetings.

2. Meeting host

As the leader of your group, you may also end up serving as the meeting host. But a way to involve others is recruiting someone else to host the meeting.

3. Food coordinator

While this seems like a relatively minor detail, meeting refreshments can become a major distraction for you to keep up with. Chances are, at least one person in your group would love to take this responsibility off your shoulders, and that person will be uniquely gifted to handle this duty with grace.

4. Child-care coordinator

Because child care can be a big issue for your group, let someone with the contacts, know-how, and a heart for kids help address this vital issue.

CROSS REFERENCE:
"6 Small Group Child-Care Solutions," Section 1, page 25

5. "Inreach" coordinator

Over the course of your group's time together, specific needs inevitably will arise within the group. For example, someone could get sick and need meals, or the group may want to send a card of encouragement. An "inreach" coordinator takes charge of many details, such as picking up birthday and get well cards that the group can send and arranging for meals.

6. Outreach coordinator

Some people have a way of connecting with newcomers. A healthy, open group should desire to see others join and experience Christian community. While everyone in the group is encouraged to reach out to others, let this person take the lead in promoting the group and making visitors feel welcome.

7. Subgroup leader(s)

Depending on the size of your group, you may find it very helpful and practical to break into smaller groups at various points in a meeting. This is a great opportunity to let leaders lead and to help develop future leaders as well.

15 TOOLS EVERY LEADER NEEDS

Good carpenters need fully stocked toolboxes. Without tools, their hands are tied, no matter how skilled they may be. Small group leaders also require a certain set of tools. You'll use some tools all the time; others might be tucked away in your toolbox, accessible but not immediately needed.

1. The study or lesson

It is a scary thing to arrive at your meeting and realize that you forgot to prepare to lead the study. "Winging it" often results in misguided discussion and the sharing of ignorance. Even more important than bringing the lesson is knowing the content of the lesson. You must study the lesson so you can know the material and communicate it effectively. Leaders who understand the material have a greater ability to help people apply it to their lives and even adapt it to meet specific needs.

2. An icebreaker or warm-up

Group members arrive each week with many different things on their minds: traffic jams, unruly kids, frustration about work, and so forth. People don't have an innate ability to jump right into a deep discussion about spiritual things. They need to warm up to spiritual conversation. They need to be prepared to reveal their heart to others. This is the purpose of a warm-up or icebreaker.

You can break the ice in one of two ways. You can strike up casual conversation as people arrive, asking people questions like, "What did you do today?" "How was work?" or "You told me (insert specific situation). How did that go?" A second approach is more formal. To start off the meeting, you can ask an icebreaker question. Some examples: "What would be your ideal vacation?" "Who was your hero when you were growing up?" "When you retire, what do you want to do?"

CROSS REFERENCE:
"10 Easy Warm-Ups," Section 1, page 32

3. Worship songs

If your group worships together, choose the songs before the meeting starts. You don't want to be thinking about such things as people are arriving, because it could communicate that you don't care about your group members. Many group leaders delegate the leading of worship to a musically gifted group member. If you do, you should still communicate with the worship leader before the group meeting to make sure that all is in order. Some groups sing to songs recorded on a CD or audiocassette—make sure that you have those ready.

CROSS REFERENCE:
"14 Ideas for Small Group Worship Times," Section 5, page 145

4. Worship sheets

Make sure that every small group member has a copy of the words for the worship songs. Pass these out every week, even when everyone knows the songs. That way, if you have visitors, they won't face the embarrassing situation of sitting in silence while all of the "insiders" sing at the top of their lungs to memorized songs.

5. CD player

If your group worships with the help of a worship CD, make sure that the host has a good CD player. Arrive before other members and cue the songs for the night so that your focus can be on the people in your group.

6. Your heart

You can do everything right as a leader. You can prepare the lesson, organize the worship, and make sure everything is arranged, but these are ancillary to your engaged heart. If you don't prepare and bring your heart, people see it. They know the difference between a leader who's just doing a job and one who really cares. Leading a group isn't just another chore to accomplish each week. It's a calling—a lifestyle of caring for God's people.

> **CROSS** REFERENCE:
> "40 Questions to Help You Stay Spiritually Focused," Section 1, page 50

7. The presence of Christ

Jesus said, "For where two or three come together in my name, there am I with them" (Matthew 18:20). You can stock your leadership belt with the highest-quality tools, but if you fail to use the tool that matters the most, you fail. You can easily rely on top-quality, published small group study guides and worship CDs that make it easy to sing together. But good lessons and great singing don't change lives. Jesus does. He promised to be present with those who meet in his name.

8. Extra study guides

If your group is working through a published study guide, have two or three extra copies for unexpected guests. This helps with the process of connecting them to the activities of the group.

9. List of group members

Keep an updated list of current group members with names, phone numbers, e-mail addresses, and birthdays.

10. Prayer list

You may have your own method for keeping prayer requests, but if not, use a blank sheet of paper to list all the names of your small group members, leaving space after each name. Write down prayer needs that you learn of during the group's meetings or in other conversations. It's best to write down these needs as they are shared so you don't forget the specifics.

11. Calendar

Bringing your calendar allows you to easily make arrangements to connect with group members during the week and to set dates for future group gatherings.

12. Directions to the location of next week's meeting

If your small group moves from house to house, you will want to have copies of a map to the next meeting's host home. This makes it easier for newcomers. It also lessens the need to call people the night before the meeting to tell them where you'll be meeting.

13. Greeting cards

Go to a greeting card store and stock up on birthday cards. Send cards to group members for their birthdays or give the cards to them at the meeting. Purchase a few blank cards so you can write personal words of encouragement. When someone is vulnerable and shares something especially personal in the group, write a quick note after the meeting, thanking that person for what he or she shared, and drop it in the mail the next morning.

14. Report

Many churches ask small group leaders to complete reports to turn in to the pastor or the church's lay leadership. This helps church leaders know how to support your ministry and help you care for the people in your group. You'll do a better job of completing this report accurately if you discipline yourself to do this right after your group's meeting.

15. A friend

A person isn't really a tool, but it's good for the group when you bring someone new. New people bring life and add vitality to your group. Because people are apprehensive about breaking into an established group, inviting someone may not be enough. Go pick up your friend, and use the time in the car to help him or her feel more comfortable.

13 GREAT WAYS TO WELCOME NEW MEMBERS

A successful small group experience is often the key to keeping a person in a church. But breaking into and becoming part of a new small group is tough to do. It takes determination to break into an already established group—especially if the group is tightly knit. One church adopted the theme, "Our Church Can Be Your Home." Consider making "Our Small Group Can Be Your Home" the theme of your group—and then use the following ideas to help assimilate new people into the family.

1. Photo dossier

When you enter a new group, it's tough to keep everyone's names straight. To simplify the new member's process of melding into the group, print a dossier of the group. Create a booklet or several pages stapled together that show a photo of each member (just a candid shot taken at a group meeting) and his or her name. Also list a bit of information about each person, such as where he or she works, hobbies, family (including ages of kids), and so forth.

2. Dinner on us

As the group leader, it's especially important for you to get to know new members. So take the new member out to dinner (include the spouse, even if he or she does not attend the group). Or have the new member's family over to your home for dinner. Not only will you get to know this person better, but he or she will feel comfortable with you. The connection with you will draw the individual back to the group even if he or she has a hard time connecting with other members. You can also invite one or two core members of the group to join you for dinner—as long as you make sure the focus is on getting to know the new person.

3. Group gift

Give the new person a mug (perhaps filled with chocolates and with a helium balloon attached), a T-shirt, or some other item with the small group's name on it.

4. Mini library

If your small group studies books, give new members a copy of the book you're currently studying. Expand your ministry by giving them copies of the previous book (or two) so they can see what the group has been learning about.

5. New members' reception

Every quarter, have a reception honoring all of your new group members and their families. Plan the reception as an evening where group members can focus on getting to know those who are new. Depending on the size of your group or church, this can be done by a single group, by several groups together, or as a churchwide event.

6. Adopt a member

Each time new people join your small group, recruit seasoned members to adopt them. The adoption can last for a month, six weeks, or longer. The adopter helps new members fit in—sitting by them for a few weeks, introducing them to others, getting to know them well enough to help them connect with others, perhaps even seeing the new people outside of the group meetings, and praying for them. You can also sit with new group members during church services. If they're new to the church, introduce them to others who aren't in your small group.

7. Wear name tags

For the first few weeks after new members join the group, ask other group members to wear name tags so new members can start putting faces and names together. You can facilitate this process by using people's names. For example, if you call upon a member to answer a question, you might say, "Bob, what do you think about the phrase the psalmist uses?"

8. Do your homework

This is a step you should do automatically when a new member enters the group. The week following the member's first visit, find out anything you can about the new member—check with the church office or call the person who invited the new member. Try to learn a piece of personal information you can draw on in your next conversation.

9. Gift basket

A gift basket can include a snack or specialty coffee or two, a small flower pot and seeds, or a candle, along with a Bible or other Bible study help. If the small group member is also new to the church, include information about all the ministries in the church and a copy of the church directory, as well as a copy of the contact information for the members of your small group.

You could also ask each small group member to donate an item for the gift basket. Put the member's name on a tag attached to the item—you could even create gift tags with the giver's photo on it.

10. A sweet welcome

The week after a new member comes to your group, assign someone to "mug" the person (leave a mug full of goodies on the front step along with a note welcoming the person to the group) or to drop off a tin of cookies. The person doesn't have to stick around—he or she can drop off the gift and leave.

11. Say "Thanks for coming"

Send a card to new members thanking them for gracing your group with their presence. It's even better if you have other small group members sign the card. Then drop it in the mail so the new members receive the card that week.

12. Video tour of the group

This is an expansion on the idea of creating a photograph-focused directory for new members. Create a video and have one or more guides give a "tour" of your small group, explaining procedures, purpose of the group, and so forth. Then have group members give their names and tell a bit about themselves. You could also include footage from the group's past events and fellowship times if you like. You can also include special effects—add background music, or put on the screen the name of the person who's speaking. You can include images of group members at work, doing ministry, at home with their families. Your only limit is your imagination.

13. Now appearing on the screen

Create a computer version of the video tour. Give each new member a CD of the group. Besides the photos or a video tour, you could also include notes from recent meetings, a PowerPoint presentation, a directory to download, e-mail links to group member Web sites, or whatever you want to include!

4 BEST ENDINGS FOR SMALL GROUPS

Chances are, you can find all kinds of information on starting a small group. But you might not find much written on how to end a group. Yet all good things must come to an end—so consider these suggestions for how your small group will end.

1. Begin with the end in mind

If you lead a relatively typical small group, you'll start to feel like a family. You'll share each other's joys and struggles and bear one another's burdens in your small group community. As you do, you'll grow to love one another deeply. It will be hard to end your group—unless you start the group with the end in mind. Think through the "term" of your group from the outset and let prospective participants know what they're committing to if they become part of the small group. For example:

- a six-week primer on the essentials of the faith

- a six-month short-term mission service group

- a one-year book study for young married couples

- a topical series or book of the Bible study

2. Pass the leadership baton

It's said that there's no success without a successor. Encourage your group to succeed by keeping an eye out for an individual or couple who are both gifted and willing to serve in an apprentice leader role. Let's say you've found an apprentice couple to mentor. The group needs to know that the couple have stepped forward, and the couple need an opportunity to practice what you're teaching them. Let them take the lead once a month (you might appreciate the breather!). Down the road, if God sets your ministry sights elsewhere, this couple will be well prepared to receive the leadership baton.

3. Plan for a birth announcement

Small groups are great places for spiritual growth to occur. Should God grow your group numerically as well, another ending option is that the apprentice couple lead a new group "birthed" from your group. You might put a tentative timeline of eighteen months on this step, yet always be sensitive to the Holy Spirit's lead. He may indicate through numbers and opportunity that it's time to do this sooner rather than later. In birthing a new group, encourage members to seek God's direction as to which group they'll meet with. They may select one or the other group based on location, topics, their own gift mix, and their potential to contribute to one of the groups.

4. Plan to birth several small groups

Group leaders who champion not only "inreach" (ministering to one another) but outreach (sharing the gospel) may find that God sends numerous group members as well as various apprentice leaders their way. If this is the case with you, it may be an indication that God wants to use you to launch several groups. In such cases, you'll not only serve as a small group leader, but also as a trainer of future leaders in the spirit of 2 Timothy 2:2.

3 WAYS TO GAUGE IF IT'S TIME TO END YOUR GROUP

If you're thinking that it may be time to end your small group, make sure you're listening to the right voice. Is it exhaustion? Is it frustration? Is it truly God's direction? How can you know for sure?

1. Pray for wisdom

"If any of you lacks wisdom, he should ask God, who gives generously to all without finding fault, and it will be given to him" (James 1:5).

2. Yield your heart

"Therefore, I urge you, brothers, in view of God's mercy, to offer your bodies as living sacrifices, holy and pleasing to God—this is your spiritual act of worship. Do not conform any longer to the pattern of this world, but be transformed by the renewing of your mind. Then you will be able to test and approve what God's will is—his good, pleasing and perfect will" (Romans 12:1-2).

3. Ask, seek, and knock

"Ask and it will be given to you; seek and you will find; knock and the door will be opened to you. For everyone who asks receives; he who seeks finds; and to him who knocks, the door will be opened" (Matthew 7:7-8).

11 STEPS TO TAKE WHEN YOU KNOW IT'S TIME TO GO

If God seems to be confirming that it's time to pursue an appropriate ending for your group, commit to do so in such a way that glorifies God and affirms others. The following considerations will help you to do this.

1. Talk to your church leaders

Inform them about how God is leading you, ask for their advice, and put it into practice.

2. Let your small group know

Of course, you need to seek an appropriate time to do this—at least several weeks before you're leaving. Be prepared to allow time for group members to process the implications of having new leaders.

3. Ask the group to help you "go out with a bang"

Call a special meeting to plan what that might look like. Have a party or cookout or potluck. If the group is becoming two or more groups, you might have a launching celebration instead of an ending party.

4. Have an "end of the group" prayer meeting

Thank God for what he's done through the small group, what he continues to do in the life of each member, and his commitment to use each one in his service.

5. Provide assurances

Let group members know that you'll never stop being committed to their success in the Lord.

6. Conduct a wrap-up session

Spend the final meeting of your group evaluating how the group has grown. Also discuss what worked and what didn't—even what you need to remember when saying yes to small group leadership in the future.

7. Keep praying for one another

Prayer is a habit you've practiced week after week, and you have special insight into the needs of your group because you've walked with them for some time. So keep things going. Commit to pray for everyone in the group, perhaps one day a week. If you don't have specific prayer requests, perhaps that's your cue to contact them.

8. Keep in touch with one another

There are many quick ways to do this. Send an e-mail update and ask what's going on in their worlds. Send cards or handwritten notes; in this "e-connected" world, a personal note can have more of an effect than you realize. Invite group members to have coffee or a meal from time to time. How about going to an event together, such as a Christian concert or football game?

9. Get together three or four times a year

It doesn't have to be anything special. Establish a tradition of watching the Super Bowl together, gather for an Independence Day barbecue and fireworks show, play board games by the fire in the fall, or hold a Christmas open house and carol sing.

10. Hold an annual reunion

Invite everyone who has ever attended your small group to come together once again to touch base. Of course, have a meal together and give people time to visit informally. But then come together and go around the room to give people an opportunity to update the group with what's going on in their lives. Questions to get you going include "What are you most excited about these days?" "What's your biggest challenge?" "Can you take a few minutes to update us on some of the prayer requests we prayed for when we met regularly?"

11. Let group members know that you're available

If you're willing to do so, be available for group members should the need arise. Your commitment doesn't stop at the door of the group's last meeting! Communicate that your door is always open.

SHAKE UP
Easy Ways to Breathe Energy Into a Stagnant Group

Shake Up—
Easy Ways to Breathe Energy Into a Stagnant Group

If your small group seems to be slipping into an easy groove, or if group members are losing interest, it might be time to shake things up. This could be as simple as changing the location where your group meets, planning some creative activities, or adding fun by having a movie night.

18 IDEAS FOR PLACES TO MEET

Your group might decide to meet in a new location just because it's different—or you might meet somewhere that will help stress a point of a lesson. Consider these alternatives to where you're meeting now.

1. Members' homes

If you regularly meet at your church, meeting in group members' homes can be a welcome change, offering several benefits. Almost any home is warmer than the nicest church meeting room. You can tend to foster more intimacy in a home. Ask someone else to bring refreshments so the host only has to be concerned about getting the house ready. Encourage your host not to feel he or she has to have a perfectly clean home before the group can come.

2. Park it!

Take advantage of nice weather by meeting in a park. Even though you're meeting in a park, think twice before inviting group members to bring their kids. Chances are, you'll lose members several times during the meeting as they go check on their children. If you decide to use a shelter at the park, be sure to follow procedures for scheduling it ahead of time.

3. Coffee, tea, or Bible study?

Meet in a coffee shop for a change of pace. Let group members purchase coffee or snacks, drag some tables together, and go for it. This works especially well if you have a local coffee house owned by a Christian group or church.

4. True combination meal

Go to a casual restaurant for a combo meal—food and Bible study. This might work best if you choose a place like a deli—where everyone orders what they want from a counter and sits together. If the location has a separate room, you may want to reserve it.

5. Study the Book in a store

Most chain bookstores and many local ones have a place where meetings can be held—even if in overstuffed chairs in the middle of the store. Schedule with the store to be sure it's OK to hold your group meeting there. Some Christian bookstores and local libraries also have meeting rooms you can reserve.

6. Local attractions

Does your city have a favorite attraction that might be fun to meet at? It could be man-made, like a special plaza, or natural, like a beach. Or how about the café inside a museum? These can offer fun places to meet for a change.

7. Walking on the water

Walk around on the water by using a pontoon boat—or any other boat that will hold your group. Combine a riverboat ride with a journey into Scripture—the Bible is full of meaningful references to water that you can explore.

8. Ride the rails

Take a train ride. Fill a passenger car with your group. This works especially well if the train travels to a certain point and then returns over the same terrain. Enjoy the tour on the way there, and enjoy a Bible study or prayer and praise time on the way back to the station.

9. In the middle of commerce

Try meeting in a mall, at the food bar in a grocery store or superstore, or in another shopping area where places are available for just hanging around.

10. Out on the farm

Getting back to nature can be a great place to discuss the themes of reaping, sowing, growth, and harvest.

11. Step into history

Do you have any historic landmarks nearby? Tie in a tour of the historic location with a lesson. Perhaps it's a battle site—prepare a lesson about taking a stand, fighting for what we believe in, or the price of freedom. At a historic home, you could discuss people of the past and the challenges they faced.

12. Amusement park

What about spending a day together at an amusement park? At lunchtime, grab some food and do a brief study that ties into the events of the day.

13. A view of the world

If you live in a larger city, you might want to meet in a skyscraper or gather on a hillside. Your lesson might focus on the temptations of the world.

14. Children's museum

Take time to browse around, and gather for a lesson with a focus of what it means to come to God like a child and to exhibit childlike faith.

15. Holiday sites

Does your city have some special holiday attractions? How can you use these to get away and tie in to the season? And while Christmas might be the most logical holiday to take advantage of this, it's not the only one!

16. Cemetery

A cemetery can be a good object lesson location for many studies. Talk about the brevity of earthly life. Don't let this unusual occasion create a ghoulish meeting, though. You might want to focus on the celebration of life, more than the sorrow of death, or the positive aspect of each person living for a reason and the joy of heritage.

17. Where the action is

A hub where people come and go from all over—like an airport, bus station, or train terminal—can be an interesting place to meet.

18. Sports arena

How about meeting on the diamond at an empty baseball field? Or on a tennis court that's not being used? Especially great for a lesson on competition!

22 FUN SMALL GROUP ACTIVITIES

"Our mouths were filled with laughter, our tongues with songs of joy" (Psalm 126:2).

Sounds like their small group activity was a success! With a little planning and a lot of imagination, your team can pull off a great time of fun, too. There's something about simply getting a bit crazy that bonds people like nothing else can. Most of these activities cost less than five dollars per person, and many are absolutely free. Peter said we were set aside as a "peculiar people" (1 Peter 2:9, King James Version). Loosely translated, that means going bananas every once in a while is biblical, so let's party!

1. Karaoke or really bad stand-up comedian night

"Cel-e-brate good times, come on!" Here's your chance to boogie or bewilder fellow group members with renditions of your favorite tunes or jokes. Choose someone to emcee, and have each person perform to the worst of their ability. The audience can hold up numbered index cards to rate performances. Booing and heckling are encouraged. Let the popcorn fly!

> **You'll need:**
> ✓ a microphone (working or not; for smaller groups, a simple prop is fine)
> ✓ a boombox
> ✓ music (CDs or cassettes)
> ✓ index cards and pencils
> ✓ noisemakers (horns, whistles, rattles)
> ✓ popcorn (to eat or toss at "entertainers")

2. Mystery trip

Where are you headed? Only your driver and tour guide know for sure. Leaders may give clues at their discretion, like "wear walking shoes" or "bring your swimsuit." You might head for a common local attraction or go sightseeing at a more remote location. Let group members know the time frame ("We'll be back in two hours" or "We'll be gone overnight"), but otherwise keep them in the dark as long as possible!

> **You'll need:**
> ✓ a passenger van (or church bus, depending on size of group)
> ✓ gas money
> ✓ items as instructed by your tour guide

3. Back-to-school night

This game assumes there's a mischievous fourth-grader hiding inside every adult. Have group members dress in play clothes and literally take them back to their childhood by having them play games like hopscotch, jump-rope, and dodge ball. Display elementary school pictures and awards, letting everyone figure out who's who and celebrating those early successes that made Mom so proud.

> **You'll need:**
> ✓ sidewalk chalk
> ✓ jump-ropes
> ✓ large balls
> ✓ old elementary school pictures and awards (ribbons, trophies, certificates)

4. Gifts and hobbies

It is time to honor the gifts and strengths of individual group members. Have all group members bring items that represent their favorite hobbies, like a piece of quilting or woodworking, pottery, a short story, poetry, and so forth. After each group member shares his or her creative piece and tells why this particular activity is special, clap and thank God for the unique talents he's given that person.

> **You'll need:**
> ✓ handmade items or original works

5. Song burst

Whether you're soprano, bass, alto, or tenor—or simply A (always) flat—this activity will have your group bursting out laughing. Pick a theme like "animals." As you go around the circle, each person must sing a line of a song that relates to the theme, like "Old McDonald had a pig" or "How much is that doggie in the window?" Anyone who falters has to drop out. Keep going until only one person is left who can think of a song related to the theme. If the remaining person can sing one more line, you've got a winner!

> **You'll need:**
> ✓ your singing voice

6. Digital scavenger hunt

Divide group members into teams, then pass out lists of things to find within a designated area (such as your neighborhood, town, or within a ten-mile radius). As group members locate each item, they snap a digital photo of themselves with the item. (The goofier the pose, the better, of course!) Set a time for all teams to meet back at the starting point, then compare pictures to see which team came closest to completing the list.

> **You'll need:**
> ✓ a digital camera for each team
> ✓ a list of items to locate
> ✓ transportation, depending on size of search area

7. Adult slumber parties

Remember how much fun it was to lounge around in your pajamas, watching movies and giggling and sharing secrets with your pals? Even though you're all grown up, it can still be just as much fun. Don't assume slumber parties are just for gals. Guys like this sort of thing, too, so set them up with their own slumber party in a neighboring house, or they could pitch a tent in the back yard.

> **You'll need:**
> ✓ pajamas
> ✓ sleeping bags and pillows
> ✓ snacks
> ✓ a place to crash for the night

8. Why and because

Pass out two pieces of scrap paper and a pencil to group members, asking them to write a "why" question on one piece and the proper "because" answer on another. (For example, "Why does Bill wear glasses?" and "Because he can't see without them.") Put the "why" questions in one basket, and the "because" answers in the other basket. Mix up the papers in the two separate baskets, then pull out a question and read it to the group. Have someone else choose a paper from the "because" basket and see how silly the answers turn out to be.

> **You'll need:**
> ✓ scraps of paper
> ✓ pencils
> ✓ two baskets

9. Three dollars and thirty-three cents party

Gather $3.33 from each person attending, and pool all the money into a party pot. Once you know how much the group has to work with, have everyone brainstorm ways the money can be used for something fun to do that evening.

You'll need:
✓ $3.33 per person

Maybe you can get some pizza to eat, rent a movie to watch, buy a board game to play, or purchase kites to fly. Kick your imaginations into high gear!

10. Round robin carwash

Park group members' cars in a circle in a large parking lot with access to water. Have couples wash and detail another family's automobile. For instance, Bob and Mary clean Tom and Rhonda's minivan; Tom and Rhonda wash Mike and Karen's SUV; Mike and Karen take on Bob and Mary's station wagon. Make this a labor of love as each couple tries to outdo the others. The bonus is that all the cars end up sparkling clean, inside and out. And if a water fight breaks out, that's fun, too!

You'll need:
✓ dish soap, soft cloths, and sponges
✓ garden hoses with water access
✓ buckets
✓ vacuum cleaners
✓ car interior cleaning products
✓ swimsuits and shorts

11. Progressive dinner

Progressive dinners work especially well with larger groups, say a dozen or more people. Have four volunteers offer their homes as stops on your tantalizing tour. Split the party menu into appetizers, salads, entrees, and desserts; decide which house will feature which course; then assign people to bring various dishes.

You'll need:
✓ four houses
✓ transportation
✓ food, drinks, and ice
✓ paper plates/cups, utensils, napkins

Once the dinner begins, transport drinks and unused plates, cups, and utensils from location to location. Choose houses close to each other to minimize drive time, and draft minivan owners to ferry people from one point to the next. Plan on spending about thirty to forty minutes at each location.

12. Stargazing and praising

There's no better time to spot the heavens declaring the glory of God than on a clear night, with stars sparkling and planets twirling overhead. Choose your stargazing date, then visit Internet sites like Star Date Online (www.stardate.org) to make a list of stars and planets visible to the naked eye in your part of the world that evening. Choose a dark field away from city lights, spread out blankets, and have people lie on their backs for a panoramic view of the sky above. Telescopes are nice, but not necessary. Use your lists to find and identify celestial points, and then end your stargazing with praise songs and Scripture reading (check references to the word *heavens* in a Bible concordance).

You'll need:
- ✓ a clear night
- ✓ blankets
- ✓ Internet access
- ✓ Bibles
- ✓ flashlights

13. Build-a-sundae ice cream social

To keep the line moving, have a couple of servers dish up ice cream, then direct group members to another table to add whatever fruit and toppings they desire. The key to a great sundae is keeping the main ingredient cold and fresh, so don't bring out the ice cream until right before you start scooping. If the ice cream is too hard, just warm the scoop under hot water, and then start serving.

You'll need:
- ✓ several varieties of ice cream
- ✓ fresh fruit (bananas, strawberries, blueberries, pineapple, cherries)
- ✓ toppings (nuts, chocolate/butterscotch syrup, candies, whipped cream)
- ✓ serving scoops, spoons, and bowls

14. Pizza pizazz

Mix up pizza dough prior to the party, and throw some Italian

opera music on the boombox. Have group members roll out and shape their individually sized pizza crust on a floured surface, ladle on sauce, and add preferred toppings. Bake, and *voilà*! Private homes can usually handle pizza-making groups of eight or less. Larger groups might opt for using the larger kitchens and ovens at church.

You'll need:
- ✓ pizza dough
- ✓ pizza sauce
- ✓ cheese and assorted meat and vegetable toppings
- ✓ rolling pins, pizza pans, and pizza cutters
- ✓ an oven
- ✓ a boombox

15. Screen tests

Lights! Camera! Act out famous scenes from movies (found online at sites like www.simplyscripts.com), recording your screen tests with a camcorder. After everyone does their thing, pop the

results into your VCR and rate the performances: thumbs up or thumbs down. You can choose scene themes that coincide with current small group topics. For example, if your group is studying parenting skills, try this activity

You'll need:
- ✓ a camcorder
- ✓ movie quotes
- ✓ props

featuring famous moms and dads (like Joan Crawford wigging out over wire hangers in *Mommie Dearest* or Steve Martin trying to understand wedding planner Franck in *Father of the Bride*).

16. Games night

Games night is another activity that screams "the more, the merrier." To begin, have everyone count off in threes (ones head for the first room, twos to the second, and threes to the third). Ring the bell, and group members start playing whichever game is in their particular room. After forty-five minutes, ring the bell to end the first session. Individuals can stay where they are or move to another game. After another forty-five minutes, switch again. Encourage group members to interact with different people each time.

> **You'll need:**
> ✓ three rooms, or a large area that can be split into three sections
> ✓ three interactive games that include six or more players, like Cranium, Pictionary, Scattergories, or Outburst
> ✓ a bell

Your group can also play this outdoors, using the same setup, except playing outdoor games like basketball, volleyball, and Frisbee golf.

17. Year-round caroling

Who says caroling is just for Christmas? Gather your group and song sheets for hymns or praise songs, and head for the nearest street corner to entertain passing pedestrians. Or surprise your pastor with an impromptu concert on your pastor's front lawn. Or perk up a friend who's had a rough week. Afterward, meet at one of the carolers' homes for cider, cookies, and conversation.

> **You'll need:**
> ✓ song sheets
> ✓ an acoustic guitar
> ✓ transportation

18. Seventies teen idol flashbacks

It's time to drag out those old Partridge Family and Donny Osmond posters. Turn on strobe lights, black lights, and lava lamps; slap some Jackson Five or Bee Gees on the turntable; and have your partiers don seventies threads—including love beads, fringe, and polyester. Don't forget the Happy Faces! Groovy, man.

You'll need:
- ✓ seventies costumes
- ✓ seventies music
- ✓ strobe lights, black lights, and lava lamps
- ✓ stereo

19. What I like about you

Pass out scraps of paper and pencils to group members. Ask them to write the name of each group member on a separate piece of paper, followed by something they like about that person. Encourage people to write something nice, even if they don't know the person they're writing about very well. (First impressions are still important!) When everyone finishes writing, gather the slips of paper in a basket, then pull the papers out one by one, reading the name and complimentary comment. After reading a paper, pass it to the person who was praised so he or she can keep it.

You'll need:
- ✓ scraps of paper
- ✓ pencils
- ✓ a basket

20. Watermania

Play Beach Boys surfing songs while slipping and sliding around the lawn, splashing through wading pools, and super-soaking friends with water balloons. Caution—you will get wet!

You'll need:
- ✓ garden hoses and sprinklers
- ✓ children's wading pools
- ✓ water pistols/super soakers
- ✓ water balloons
- ✓ swimsuits and shorts
- ✓ a boombox

21. Story in the round

The first person begins a story with one sentence that includes a noun or verb that starts with the letter "*a*." For example, "I was walking through the *apple* orchard the other day, when I saw something that surprised me." The second person continues the story with a

You'll need:

✓ your imagination

sentence that includes a word beginning with the letter "*b*": "There was a *boa* constrictor at the base of the largest tree." The third person continues with a sentence featuring a word beginning with "*c*": "It was all *coiled* up and ready to strike!" and so on. Continue around the circle until you end the story with a sentence containing a word beginning with "*z*."

22. Mad makeovers

In this silly hair and makeup session, you don't do your own do, your friends do your do for you—with hilarious results. Keep mirrors hidden until you reveal the new and "improved" versions of each other. To make things even more fun, include the guys and transform Prince Charmings into Prince Alarmings!

You'll need:

✓ cosmetics

✓ hair products

✓ curling irons and hair dryers

✓ mirrors

10 SMALL GROUP MOVIE NIGHTS

Another option for shaking up your group is occasionally substituting watching and discussing a movie. It's not unusual for people to want to discuss a film when it's over, but it's unusual that their thoughts on the spiritual implications come out before their evaluation of the acting, laughs, and plot.

Movies are a fun, social way to get together. People usually associate them with a free evening with nothing to do. When you pitch the idea to your group, be clear that while you want to take a break from the usual, you're also doing this to provoke thought and discussion about faith and culture. When the movie is over, offer a clear segue into the conversation, such as, "I thought we could spend some time discussing how this movie relates to the Christian faith, and so I've planned a few questions just to get us started."

Plan discussion questions that move from comfortably wide to appropriately deep. For instance, you might start with naturally broad questions like, "What did you think?" Then gradually get more specific with "What part of your own life did you see in the film?" This can lead to, "How did this movie say something about the Christian faith?" Then move on to the questions listed for each movie that follows.

One word of caution about choosing movies appropriate for your group: As a rule, avoid movies that are rated R, especially if they earned that rating for explicit sexuality or gratuitous violence. If you have an intergenerational group with children present, it's likely that some of the movies listed here wouldn't be appropriate. Always preview films for content.

M O V I E 1
Leap of Faith (1992)
Genre: *Comedy/Drama*
Run Time: *108 minutes*
Rating: *Rated PG-13 for language*

Plot : A famous evangelist, Reverend Jonas Nightingale, comes to town with his tents, his miracles, and his profiteering. Little does he know that God sometimes works despite his messengers.

Discussion Starter Questions

• Why do people follow charismatic leaders, even when they're frauds?

• What effect do preachers like Jonas have on our culture?

• How has God made surprise appearances in your life?

• What do you think of the message of Philippians 1:15-18 in relation to this film?

MOVIE 2
Shadowlands (1993)

Genre: *Drama/Romance*
Run Time: *131 minutes*
Rating: *Rated PG*

Plot: The story joins the life of C.S. Lewis late, after he has established himself as an internationally known Christian writer, speaker, and professor. However, young love enters his life via Joy Gresham. Lewis goes through the passion of love and the agony of loss as Joy succumbs to cancer. Lewis walks us through the experience of faith in suffering.

Discussion Starter Questions
• How do you think Lewis's faith changed during these years?

• How has your faith changed in the midst of suffering?

• Why does God allow us to go through times like these?

• What's the significance of Hebrews 2:9-10 in relation to trials like these?

• What difference does it make that Jesus suffered as we do?

Movie Night

MOVIE 3

My Life **(1993)**

Genre: *Drama*

Run Time: *117 minutes*

Rating: *Rated PG-13 for mature themes (questionable for children), profanity*

Plot: Bob Jones learned as a young boy that you don't always get what you pray for. But now, as an adult, Bob is diagnosed with cancer and once again prays with the faith of a child for the one thing he wants most—that he'll live long enough to see his own child born. He sets out to videotape all the advice he most wants to give his child.

Discussion Starter Questions

• What can we pray for?

• How does God work through our prayers?

• If you wanted to leave behind a tape of what you thought was most important in life, what kinds of things would you include?

• Read some of Paul's last words in 2 Timothy 4:6-8. What might make someone's final thoughts so confident?

MOVIE 4

Minority Report (2002)

Genre: *Action/Sci-fi*

Run Time: *145 minutes*

Rating: *Rated PG-13 for violence, brief language, some sexuality, and drug content*

Plot: In a futuristic world, the police have developed a method of predicting crime and arresting criminals before they do the deed. Crime is disappearing, but there's one major ethical dilemma: What does it mean to punish people who haven't yet done anything wrong? What if you were wrong? And would you still trust the system if you suddenly discovered that you were guilty of a crime you had yet to commit?

Discussion Starter Questions

• Do you think people should be arrested if someone knows they will inevitably commit a crime in the future? Explain.

• If God plans the course of our lives, how can we be held responsible for the things we do?

• Would you rather be free from fear of crime or be free to do what you want?

• According to Galatians 5:13-14, what should we do with our freedom? How risky was it for God to give us such freedom?

MOVIE 5

The Count of Monte Cristo (2002)

Genre: *Action/Drama*

Run Time: *131 minutes*

Rating: *Rated PG-13 for adventure violence/swordplay and some sensuality*

Plot: When Edmond Dantes is betrayed by a friend and unjustly jailed, he spends his imprisonment planning for sweet revenge. Emerging as a social elite, he wins the heart of his old love, reclaims his place in society, and finally confronts the traitor.

Discussion Starter Questions

• What makes revenge so hard to let go of?

• How would God want us to deal with serious betrayal in our lives?

• How has God led you through betrayal by a friend?

• How might our world change if Christians more consistently applied Jesus' teaching in Matthew 5:38-42?

MOVIE 6
Les Misérables (1998)

Genre: *Drama*

Run Time: *134 minutes*

Rating: *Rated PG-13 for mild violence and some sexual content*

Plot: Jean Valjean leaves prison and builds a new life, but is doggedly pursued by a police officer named Javert who is intent on following the letter of the law. In the midst of being hunted, Jean dedicates himself to rescuing a young lady.

Discussion Starter Questions

• Why does the priest protect Jean Valjean?

• What purpose does God's law serve in our lives?

• Does God's law ever feel too legalistic? When does it feel forgiving?

• Why does Paul describe the law as he does in Galatians 3:10-11?

What Dreams May Come (1998)

Genre: *Drama/Fantasy*
Run Time: *113 minutes*
Rating: *Rated PG-13 for adult themes*

Plot: Chris is killed in a car accident, only to discover that there is life on the other side. He finds himself separated from but still connected to the wife whom he loved. The movie is a colorful fantasy about what the afterlife might look like, and while it is not written from a biblical perspective, it awakens provocative ideas to stimulate our imaginations about heaven.

Discussion Starter Questions

• How were these images similar to and different from your own view of the afterlife?

• What is there to be gained from speculating about what life after death will be like?

• What about life after death can we look forward to? What should concern us?

• What do you think of the promises contained in Revelation 21:1-4?

MOVIE 8
Shallow Hal (2001)
Genre: *Comedy*
Run Time: *113 minutes*
Rating: *Rated PG-13 for language and sexual content*

Plot: Hal is a man who only sees women on the outside, ignoring character for the sake of physical attraction. When an inspirational speaker changes Hal's worldview, he falls in love with a woman who is different from the type of girls he has always tried to date. He sees Rosemary as the beautiful woman that she is and in the process has to re-evaluate his shallow view of the world.

Discussion Starter Questions

• How are your views of other people shaped by biases about attraction?

• What would your life be like if you saw people's character before their physical appearance?

• How does God want us to see people of the opposite sex?

• How does Galatians 2:6 bear on this discussion?

MOVIE 9
The Mission (1986)
Genre: *Drama*
Run Time: *126 minutes*
Rating: *Rated PG*

Plot: Two Jesuit priests and friends wrestle over Jesus' teachings on love and enemies as they try to preserve a mission in South America.

Discussion Starter Questions

• What causes would you be willing to give your life for?

• Which priest do you think acted as Jesus would have him act? Why?

• What do you think the life of a missionary is like today?

• How do you respond to Jesus' teaching in Matthew 10:37-39?

MOVIE 10
A Christmas Story (1983)
Genre: *Comedy*
Run Time: *94 minutes*
Rating: *Rated PG*

Plot: Ralph wants a BB gun more than anything else for Christmas, but it doesn't look like Santa, his parents, or anyone else is going to come through for him. In the meantime, he's learning everything a nine-year-old needs to know about family, traditions, and hope.

Discussion Starter Questions

• What traditions were most important in your family?

• What was one memorable life lesson you learned as a child from your family?

• How does God work through the simple, mundane details of family life?

• Why do you think Paul make such a strong statement about family in 1 Timothy 5:8?

DEEP AND WIDE
Ways to Get to Know Each Other Better

SECTION 4: Table of Contents

④

SECTION 4: Deep and Wide

Deep and Wide—
Ways to Get to Know Each Other Better

Remember when someone asked Jesus which commandment was the greatest? "Loving God," he answered. And then he added: "And the second is like it: 'Love your neighbor as yourself'" (Matthew 22:39).

It's one thing to say you love God and others, but how is that reflected in day-to-day life? Small groups are excellent places to process and live out a life of love.

42 PRACTICAL WAYS TO SHOW YOU CARE

Sometimes it's easy to feel like people in the large group (the church) hardly know you or your needs at all. But your small group provides people a chance to share what's really going on in their lives and to hear what's really going on in others' lives. In the course of these conversations, practical needs surface. Learning of these needs offers all members of your small group opportunities to care for one another in practical ways.

1. Listen to what people say. And pay attention to what they're saying beyond their words through nonverbal communication, which accounts for most of what a person communicates!

2. Show that you're paying attention by repeating back what you hear. Take note of the needs that surface. Express your commitment to give further attention—to "be there" to listen some more.

3. Know when to speak and when to remain silent. Sometimes "silence is golden." Give others a listening ear rather than an earful of advice.

4. Use humor appropriately, to build up and not to demean.

5. Extend grace to one another.

6. Reflect humility.

7. Show up on time (or even be a couple minutes early).

8. Keep your word. Do what you say you'll do.

9. Tell the truth. Be a person of integrity.

10. Be willing to serve as a personal reference (such as for someone seeking a job).

11. Be willing to be a mediator to help resolve conflict in a biblical and God-honoring manner (see Matthew 18).

CROSS REFERENCE:
"7 Basic Ways to Deal With Problems in Your Group," Section 2, page 64

12. Show that you care with appropriate touch—a handshake or a hug.

13. Allow someone to serve you.

14. Sacrificially spend time with another group member.

15. Do things together, such as going to the zoo, a movie, shopping with one another.

16. Give someone a ride somewhere.

17. Go along with a group member who has a difficult appointment (for example, a doctor's visit).

18. Be there to "rejoice with those who rejoice; mourn with those who mourn" (Romans 12:15).

19. Go out for a meal or coffee, simply to spend time together. Quality time happens in the midst of quantity time.

20. Jot a note or send a card, not merely on special occasions but for no reason at all.

21. Remember and take time out to celebrate special occasions, such as birthdays, anniversaries, graduations, and so forth.

CROSS REFERENCE:
"5 Ready-to-Go Special Occasion Bible Studies," Section 6, page 156

22. If a group member says, "Pray for me," consider doing so right then and there.

23. Pray when you say you're going to pray for someone.

24. What do you do for work? How can you give your services to others in the group?

25. What are your hobbies? Do you work on cars? Are you good at crafts? Whatever it is that you have and do, use it all to help others.

26. What unique abilities do you have? Someone who can write or edit can help an out-of-work group member put together a résumé. Paint? Pull weeds? Lift boxes?

27. If you play guitar, be willing to lead songs of praise and worship in your group.

28. Serve food at group meetings and fellowship times.

29. Clean a group member's house.

30. Help someone from the group move.

31. Baby-sit a group member's kids to give Mom a break or a couple a night out.

32. Err on the side of showing hospitality.

33. You may not be able to meet a particular need (such as car repair or hemming up a dress), but can you be a "networker" who connects a skilled person to help meet a group member's need?

34. Bring a meal to a group member in need (such as a new mother).

35. Help someone from the group with a financial gift, even anonymously.

36. Lend money to meet an emergency need without charging interest.

37. Give or lend clothes, furniture, a car, or other possessions, as needed.

38. Open your home to a member of the group in need of an extended stay.

39. Give a group member a Bible, an inspirational book, or a Christian CD as a demonstration of encouragement.

40. Encourage a fellow group member with a particular Bible verse or passage.

41. Give a gift for no reason at all.

42. Sell something of value in order to sacrificially help meet the needs of others.

13 WAYS TO LIVE OUT "ONE ANOTHERS"

The New Testament is full of guidance on how to treat people. One set of relationship-oriented verses is called the "one anothers." While they sound good, it can sometimes be difficult to put them into practice. Here are some ideas on how members of your small group can live out Scripture's "one another" passages.

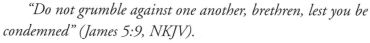

1. No grumbling allowed

"Have peace with one another" (Mark 9:50, New King James Version).

"Do not grumble against one another, brethren, lest you be condemned" (James 5:9, NKJV).

Sign a group covenant or simply agree together to not allow gossip, bickering, complaining, or cliques within the group.

2. Don't let conflict fester

"Bearing with one another, and forgiving one another" (Colossians 3: 13, NKJV).

In your group covenant, establish how you'll handle disagreements between group members. It's better to work things out as soon as possible—even if it's awkward to do so—than to let disagreements, anger, and resentment fester. You might also include a statement about respecting each person's opinion and right to talk. Allow people with differing opinions to each share their side. If conflict occurs, encourage group members to work things out between themselves without bringing other group members into the disagreement.

CROSS REFERENCE:

"13 Items to Consider Including in a Group Covenant," Section 2, page 61

3. Look for ways to serve

"You also ought to wash one another's feet" (John 13:14, NKJV).
"Submit to one another" (Ephesians 5:21).

Taken literally, you could hold a feet-washing ceremony during one of your meetings. This humble act toward others will help establish respect, intimacy, and openness among the members of your group and will help to draw them closer. On a broader scale, use this principle to be constantly looking for ways to serve each other—not to gain recognition, but simply to offer yourselves to one another in service.

4. Demonstrate unconditional love

"Love one another; as I have loved you, that you also love one another" (John 13:34, NKJV).

"All will know that you are My disciples, if you have love for one another" (John 13:35, NKJV).

"Love one another as I have loved you" (John 15:12, NKJV).

"Love one another" (John 15:17, NKJV).

"For you yourselves are taught by God to love one another" (1 Thessalonians 4:9, NKJV).

"Love one another fervently with a pure heart" (1 Peter 1:22, NKJV).

Get the point? We're to love each other unconditionally. In your small group, you can accomplish this by making a point of befriending the person in your group who's always in the background. Talk to him or her, exchange phone numbers, and invite the person out for coffee or a walk. Or if someone is having a bad day/week/month, stop by his or her house with some cheery flowers, homemade treats, or a funny movie. Finally, encourage friendships among group members. Pair people up as prayer partners, encouragement partners, accountability partners, Bible study partners…whatever type of relationship your group would like to establish. Get members talking to and meeting with each other outside of the established group time.

5. Demonstrate kindness

"Be kindly affectionate to one another with brotherly love, in honor giving preference to one another" (Romans 12:10, NKJV).

At each meeting, try to do something for another person in the group in a way that Jesus would. This can be as simple as letting another person have the last doughnut that you were reaching for, or inviting someone out for dinner after the group meeting.

6. Give without obligating others

"Owe no one anything except to love one another" (Romans 13:8, NKJV).

If someone in your group has a need, come together to help meet that need without expecting anything in return. Gather food or money, offer child care or a ride, bring dinner or cleaning supplies to that member's house, and offer it free of obligation.

7. Make visitors feel welcome

"Receive one another, just as Christ also received us" (Romans 15:7, NKJV).

Unless there's a compelling reason not to—such as in an established support group where trust is essential—welcome newcomers to your group.

8. Make everyone else feel welcome

"Greet one another with a holy kiss" (Romans 16:16, NKJV).

OK, maybe group members won't kiss each other as they arrive, but they can make each other feel welcome and comfortable. Greet people warmly at the door when they arrive. Have places for people to lay coats, hats, and purses. Have seating areas set up ahead of time, and set out refreshments. Consider lighting some scented candles, or think of other sensory ideas to establish a warm and welcoming environment for your group.

9. Take care of those who are "down"

"That there should be no schism in the body, but that the members should have the same care for one another" (1 Corinthians 12:25, NKJV).

"Through love serve one another" (Galatians 5:13, NKJV).

"Let us not become conceited, provoking one another, envying one another" (Galatians 5:26, NKJV).

"Bear one another's burdens" (Galatians 6:2, NKJV).

"Therefore comfort one another" (1 Thessalonians 4:18, NKJV).

It's pretty easy to spot times when you can live out these "one anothers."

- For grieving families: Provide dinner, an activity to help take their mind off their grief for a little while, a listening ear, and relief from the pressure of things that need to be done. Realize that they'll be distracted and down, so call to remind them that you hope they'll be at your next meeting, but don't try to force them to cheer up. Ask about the loved one who died and allow them to share stories, even if that happens through tears. Forget about trying to offer words of comfort—they're often clichéd phrases that don't help grieving people. Instead, just express your sorrow over their loss and offer your love.

- For families with new babies: Offer to provide meals, housecleaning, lawn mowing, and any other maintenance chores that get pushed aside when a newborn takes precedence. Offer to come and watch the baby at their house for an hour or two so the parents can get some much-needed rest. Find out if the family is lacking in any of the many basic things a baby needs.

- For families who've lost a job: Straight-out offers of cash may be difficult to accept, so look for other ways of providing for unemployed people's needs. Collect money and buy the family grocery-store gift certificates, gas cards, paper for printing out résumés, and other practical items.

CROSS REFERENCE:

"5 Ready-to-Go Special Occasion Bible Studies," Section 6, page 156

10. Honor God with your words

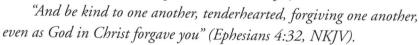

"Let each one of you speak truth with his neighbor, for we are members of one another" (Ephesians 4:25, NKJV).

"And be kind to one another, tenderhearted, forgiving one another, even as God in Christ forgave you" (Ephesians 4:32, NKJV).

"Speak to one another with psalms, hymns and spiritual songs" (Ephesians 5:19).

"Do not lie to one another" (Colossians 3:9, NKJV).

"Admonish one another" (Romans 15:14, NKJV).

In your group covenant, make it clear that group members may confront other members about behavior or speech, but this absolutely must be done in a loving way. God says we must be able to admonish or caution others, but it needs to be done in a careful and sensitive way.

CROSS REFERENCE:

"13 Items to Consider Including in a Group Covenant," Section 2, page 61

11. Remember each other between meetings

"Comfort each other and edify one another" (1 Thessalonians 5:11, NKJV).

"Exhort one another daily" (Hebrews 3:13, NKJV).

Send notes of encouragement to other people in the group for no reason other than to say you're thinking about them and praying for them. Record and mark important dates in people's lives, such as birthdays, anniversaries, new jobs, graduations, and so on.

12. Be there for each other

"Not forsaking the assembling of ourselves together, as is the manner of some, but exhorting one another" (Hebrews 10:25, NKJV).

Keep your meeting time sacred! Don't allow the busyness of life to split your group members apart; commit to be present at every meeting.

13. Pray for each other

"Confess your trespasses to one another, and pray for one another" *(James 5:16, NKJV).*

Always pray for one another. Sometimes sharing prayer requests can turn into a long time of talking—even taking time from other group activities. But don't eliminate it. Sharing prayer needs and praying for each other does wonders to establish bonds between people.

CROSS REFERENCE:

"13 Items to Consider Including in a Group Covenant," Section 2, page 61

50 QUESTIONS TO DEEPEN GROUP RELATIONSHIPS

One of the best ways we can get to know each other is by asking questions. Of course, we're more willing to open up and be honest with people we know. But developing deep and trusting relationships takes more than asking "What's your name?" "Where are you from?" or "What do you do for a living?"

To help folks build stronger ties with one another, or to help those who aren't sure what to talk about with people they don't know very well, here are questions you can discuss either as a whole group or in twos or threes, to delve into who each person is. The questions are divided into categories so you can choose those that fit a topic you're discussing or a special interest of your group.

Have fun with these! A lifelong friendship may begin with a single question.

Spiritual questions

These questions emphasize the fact that even though everyone is different, in Christ we share the same faith and we all have questions about our faith.

1. Tell me the story of how you became a Christian.

2. What's the most meaningful spiritual experience you've had?

3. What's your relationship with God like right now?

4. What would you like to change about your relationship with God?

5. Explain how you imagine or picture God.

6. What questions would you like to ask God when you get to heaven?

7. What's the most meaningful Scripture passage to you and why?

8. What confuses you about God?

9. Why did you choose the church you attend?

10. How has your relationship with God changed over your life?

Relationship questions

These questions build connections and friendships among the members of your group.

11. Who's your best friend, and why are you such good friends?

12. Do you like having a lot of friends or a few very close friends? Explain.

13. Growing up, who did you consider to be your friends and why?

14. What qualities do you look for in a friend?

15. What do you need to change about yourself in order to be a better friend?

16. What would your friends say is the best thing about having you as their friend?

Marriage and family questions

Families shape us profoundly, for good or bad, and determine to a large degree what kind of person we each become. By telling others about our families, we're telling them about ourselves.

17. Tell me the story of how your spouse/you proposed.

18. What's your favorite quality about your spouse and why?

19. What's your favorite quality about each of your children and why?

20. What does your family enjoy doing together that's unique or brings you joy to see?

21. How are you and your spouse complements of each other?

22. What amazes you about your children?

23. 'Fess up—what's your favorite children's book to read aloud?

24. Why did you choose the names you gave your children?

25. What makes your family unique?

26. How does your immediate family now (you, your spouse, your children) compare to the makeup of the family you grew up in?

"Who you are" questions

While the relationships and environments around us affect our personalities, God also gives us unique qualities. These questions will help bring out each person's individuality.

27. What's your ethnic background? Is it significant to you or not? How do you express your family background?

28. What colors, things, and type of décor do you like to surround yourself with in your home?

29. What hobbies do you have, and what about them do you enjoy?

30. What was the best part about your childhood? the worst?

31. What's one of your earliest memories?

32. How do you picture your life ten, twenty, or thirty years from now?

Dreams and aspirations questions

From the time we're very young, we aim for something. Our goals can be very personal, but talking about them with others gives people a glimpse of our deepest selves.

33. As a child, what did you want to be when you grew up? How similar or different is that dream from what you really do now?

34. If you could have any job in the world, what would you want to do? Why?

35. What foreign countries would you like to visit and why?

36. If money wasn't a factor, what would you like to spend your time doing?

Fun questions

Use these questions to share fun and funny stories to get to know the members of your small group better.

37. Who's your favorite cartoon character and why?

38. What creative activities do you enjoy?

39. What's your favorite way to relax, both with others and by yourself?

40. What was your nickname as a kid? Why were you called that? Did you like it or hate it?

41. What are you better at than anyone else you know? What are you the worst at?

42. What's the craziest/stupidest/wildest thing you've ever done?

43. What's your closest brush with fame—either you being famous or the most famous person you've come into contact with?

Deep questions

Save these questions for later. They require taking a risk to trust others with very personal information. While not for the faint of heart, they'll take relationships to a whole new level.

44. What has been the most difficult time of your life?

45. What are your greatest fears?

46. What doubts or questions do you have about God?

47. What do you think about at night in the dark when you go to bed?

48. If you could sit down with God over coffee and ask him the deep and secret questions you have for him, what would you want to ask?

49. Tell something about yourself that you've never told anyone before.

50. What are you like when no one else is around—is that the time you revel in the quiet or the time you crank up the stereo and dance?

12 WAYS TO ENCOURAGE EACH OTHER OUTSIDE OF MEETINGS

Encouragement is meant to be an integral part of the church. Hebrews 3:13 reads, "Encourage one another daily, as long as it is called Today, so that none of you may be hardened by sin's deceitfulness." What would happen in your small group if each member encouraged someone else every day? The result would be stronger individuals, a stronger small group, and a stronger church! Why not try it? Use these suggestions to "encourage one another daily."

1. Follow up on prayer requests

Many times a prayer request is for an event on a specific date. Doctor appointments, medical tests, or even awkward family gatherings are some examples of things group members may request prayer for. A phone call on that day to say that you were praying and to find out how things went reminds the other person that you care.

2. Make a phone call before an event

This is similar to the previous idea, except that you call *before* the difficult experience. Make a brief phone call the evening before and let the other group member know that you'll be praying for him or her. You can even offer to pray while on the phone together.

3. Remember children

You can touch parents' hearts through their children. It's likely the children of the families in your group are involved in sports, music, and church events. Send a child a note of congratulations or recognition of a job well done. It will probably mean more to the parent than the child, but that's OK.

4. Buddy chores

Give a member of your group your assistance for a morning. Ask when you can come over and help with a task. Most jobs go better when two work together.

5. Encouragement out of nowhere

Send a fellow group member a note to encourage him or her to keep on being faithful. Include a few personalized Scripture verses. Ask the Lord to help you know when someone may need a gentle embrace.

6. Send an article or cartoon

If you see an article or cartoon that somehow relates to something going on in a group member's life, send it to him or her. A sticky note saying, "I saw this and thought of you" is all that's necessary.

7. Send flowers or a gift basket

It may be extravagant, but your care will never be forgotten.

8. Sit together

Sit together at church. Sometimes a person can feel most alone in a large crowd. Invite a fellow group member to sit with you.

9. Group project for one

Gather the whole group together to tackle a job for one. A group of people can accomplish a lot of yard work or a needed home improvement in a short time.

10. Invite someone to your child's event

Today families are scattered. Invite an older couple to your child's concert or sporting event. It will encourage them that you thought enough of them to invite them—and your child will be delighted with the extra attention.

11. Make a long-term commitment to pray

Let a group member know that you intend to pray for him or her each day or on a particular day of the week or month for a specific length of time. Consider praying for a couple's child who's away at college for the school year. Or pray each day for someone out of work until he or she finds a job. Pray for each day of someone's medical treatment.

12. Meet a financial need

God may lead you to help a small group member through a difficult time by providing a financial gift. It could be for a night out or to cover significant expenses.

DIGGING DEEPER
Fresh Ways to Foster Spiritual Growth

SECTION 5: Table of Contents

SECTION 5: Digging Deeper

⑤

Digging Deeper—
Fresh Ways to Foster Spiritual Growth

Small groups offer a lot of things: relationships, fun, fellowship, opportunities to learn the basics about who God is. And one of the primary purposes of most small groups is to encourage and facilitate spiritual growth. This section focuses on some fresh ways your small group can grow spiritually.

17 CREATIVE WAYS TO APPROACH BIBLE STUDY

The writer of Ecclesiastes accurately said, "There is nothing new under the sun" (Ecclesiastes 1:9). This concept certainly seems to ring true with Bible study—there are only so many ways you can approach your small group lessons without making things confusing or weird. Still, here are some ways you can take several age-old truths and a few ancient practices and apply them in fresh ways in the twenty-first century.

1. Deepen Scripture's meaning through metaphor

The inspired writers and recipients of Scripture were Eastern people who processed information primarily in image and metaphor. The Bible describes God as the Shepherd, Rock, fortress, living water, Bread of Life, fire, and wind, to name some. When studying a passage that portrays God with imagery, use that metaphor in your lesson. You'll be surprised how well people remember the main idea of a study when they have an image to associate it with. For example, the main idea of Psalm 93 is that God is mighty and can't be moved. God is like a rock. Bring a rock for each group member and ask, "Where do you need God to be your strength these days? In what way do you need God to be your unwavering Rock?"

2. Present sticky ideas

Unlocking the learning styles of your group members enables you to teach effectively and helps them to learn more easily. One Christian educator has identified four primary learning styles: Imaginative, Analytic, Common Sense, and Dynamic.[1] A Bible study that includes something for each learning style will engage everyone in your group.

- *Imaginative learners* instinctively ask the question "Why?" and learn best through group interaction. Teach them by integrating group discussion in every lesson.

- *Analytic learners* want the facts in an orderly manner and tend to be information-oriented. Help them learn by including well-organized summary statements, clear main points, and handouts or outlines.

- *Common sense learners* ask "So what?" and are realistic and practical to the core. Help them learn by consistently applying lessons to real life.

- *Dynamic learners* tend to ask questions that have no answers, and they love variety. Think outside the box and give them opportunities to plan fresh ways of doing group together.

3. Send summary reflections

Send a digital summary via e-mail to help group members remember the main ideas from your study. Add questions for further reflection and give a preview of what you'll be studying during the next lesson. If your church has a Web site, posting material or providing links to articles is also an option.

4. Let the translations speak

Bring three different Bible translations to your next study and ask various people to read the same passage from each. After listening to the same passage in other translations ask some questions: "What jumped out in the other translations? What did you notice different from your usual version?" Contemporary versions such as

The Message or the New Living Translation can provide a great starting point for paraphrasing the passage yourselves.

5. Learn to "listen for God"

Contemplative Bible study, or *lectio divina,* has been used in the church for hundreds of years. Recently, it's regaining popularity. Here is a brief overview:

- **Step 1.** Pray together that God will enable you to hear his voice through the Scripture you're about to read, that your group will grow comfortable with silence, and that you'll be attentive to God's leading.

- **Step 2.** Slowly read aloud a short passage of Scripture as you listen for words, phrases, or images you believe the Holy Spirit is drawing your attention to. Read the passage a second time, and then ask people to prayerfully dwell on portions that stand out to them during several moments of silence. Have them share the word, phrase, or image that grabbed them during the reading. No explanation or analysis is necessary.

- **Step 3.** Ask everyone to ponder the question, "How does this speak to my life?" After allowing time for this, ask someone to read the text again. Then share your answers to the question. This step is all about making the text personal.

- **Step 4.** Slowly read the passage again and, during another time of silence, invite members of your group to ponder and answer the question, "How is God calling me to respond to this message?" or "What action God is calling me to take?"

- **Step 5.** Move around the circle a final time, and ask group members to pray for the person on the right (or left), that God would enable him or her to respond in the way he revealed. *Note: Lectio divina* shouldn't replace analytical Bible study, but it can serve as a healthy balance to an overly intellectual approach to Scripture.

6. Let Hollywood help!

How many times have you sat in a movie theater and laughed so hard you cried or wept so unexpectedly that you looked around to see if anyone noticed? Keep a journal of movies that affected you or made a powerful point for use in Bible studies. Opening a study with a movie quote or a video clip can be a very effective introduction.

CROSS REFERENCE:

"10 Small Group Movie Nights," Section 3, page 99

7. Treat Scripture like honey

Ancient and contemporary rabbis have a special practice that you might adopt for your group. When young students receive their first copy of the Scriptures, the Torah, the rabbi solemnly hands each child a new text, places a square of wax paper on top, and drops a small dollop of honey onto it. As the students look from the honey to the rabbi, he says, "Whenever you read the text, may the Word of God always be like honey to you." Each student holds his text in one hand and touches the honey to his tongue with the other. Psalms 19:9b-10 and 119:103 set the stage for this powerful experience.

8. Picture it!

Aristotle once said, "The soul never thinks without a picture." Use images to help people learn and remember the main ideas of your lessons. Before meeting, read your passage, record the emotions and reactions the text creates, collect images that affect you in a similar way, and integrate those images into your lesson.

9. Get outdoors for fresh insights

Bring Scripture to life by noticing the natural context in which a narrative takes place, and then "transport" your group there. Some examples:

- When reading about Moses and the Red Sea crossing (Exodus 13–14), go to a nearby lake, dip your feet into the water, and read the text aloud as you discuss it on the shore afterward.

- When studying Jacob and the heavenly stairway he saw in a dream (Genesis 28), lie under the stars with a rock for your pillow, and read the text by flashlight.

- When studying Paul's message to the Athenians (Acts 17), go to a contemporary "public square" like a coffee house, shopping mall, or university and do your study in that environment. The options are limitless!

10. *Step into the Bible by acting it out*

Many portions of Scripture involve dialogue between people—sometimes even arguments and confrontation. When studying passages like these, recruit group members to act out various roles. Discuss it afterward by asking role players, "How did entering the text affect you? What did you learn?" For those who watched, ask, "What did seeing these verses acted out teach you? What did you notice from that passage that you'd never thought of before?"

11. *Make New Testament epistles come alive*

These epistles were personal letters that addressed feelings, passions, context, and real-life situations. Rewriting epistles in contemporary language is a powerful way to transport them from first century Asia Minor to the twenty-first century living room. For example, Colossians 3:21 reads "Fathers, do not embitter your children, or they will become discouraged." It could be rewritten "Fathers, love your children and discipline them firmly. But also be gentle so they learn the ways of God and are personally honored as well—not discouraged or belittled." This process creates great discussion!

12. *Awaken your mind with your hands*

Distribute small pads of paper and a can of Play-Doh and invite people to use them during the lesson. You may be surprised how some people come alive with new insights through using their hands! For example, sculpt what you think of when you picture the cup Jesus held during the Last Supper (Matthew 26:27) or the fish he roasted on the shore after his resurrection (John 21:7-9). Even the left-brained members of your group will rally around this concept after experiencing it once.

13. Make application more attainable

In every life, God wants the living Word made real. Throughout Scripture he calls for action in some way. However, application can easily become lost. Make it more attainable by asking group members to answer these questions for themselves:

- **What** action or activity is this text is calling me to?

- **When** am I going to do this?

- **Where** will this action take place in my life? (At home, on the job, during my free time, or in my quiet time.)

- **Who** will I be accountable to? (Designate prayer partners to encourage and remind each other.)

14. Receive fresh perspectives…courtesy of children

Jesus said his followers could learn much about childlike, wholehearted faith from children (Matthew 18:2-3; Mark 9:36-37; Luke 9:46-48). In the same way, your group can learn many things by listening to a child's perspectives. If you have children, read a passage with them, ask very basic questions, and record what they hear, feel, and think. Bring their responses to your session and let them spark discussion. Some will be surprising, others funny, and some startlingly accurate! If you don't have children, get permission to visit a Sunday school class at church and do the same exercise.

After hearing the children's responses, ask your group these questions:

- What did kids say that you missed?

- How will their understanding mature as they grow older?

- How does your understanding need to become more childlike?

15. Rediscover Jesus' family tree

Jesus was an actual person with real parents, grandparents, and great-grandparents. Study Jesus' genealogy (Matthew 1:1-16) and ask group members to bring family albums to the meeting. Show each other pictures of your parents and grandparents, and describe what they were like. Look up Jesus' great-grandparents and read what they were like.

Discuss:

- How did your ancestors shape who you have become?

- How has their history become yours?

- What are some ways God used Jesus' ancestors for his purposes?

16. Divide into subgroups for discussion

Some people process information best through interacting with others. Divide into subgroups of two or three (depending on the overall group's size) and give specific questions to discuss. Then come together and share your answers.

17. Grab attention by "mapping" your study

Some group members will participate more if you briefly preview your whole study at the beginning. For example, if you're leading a study of Luke 6:27-36, you could say, "After each of us reads a portion of Luke 6:27-36, I'll briefly note several of Jesus' main points. Let's use those main ideas as discussion points and imagine what it would have been like to be one of the people Jesus was talking to. I'll record your thoughts, and then we'll break up into subgroups to talk about application. Perhaps we could conclude by praying for each other regarding that personal application." You will be surprised how this benefits some people in your group.

3 GUIDELINES FOR GROUP PRAYER

CROSS REFERENCE:

"13 Approaches to Group Prayer," Section 1, page 48 and "8 Things Your Small Group can Pray For," Section 5, page 139

Prayer can become a powerful aspect of your small group. A good leader brings not only passion and experience to prayer, but also a desire to make prayer fulfilling and worthwhile for the small group.

To develop a prayer attitude like this in your group, keep these guidelines in mind.

1. Prayer isn't just about us

Of course, your group will spend time praying for group members' needs. But if your group prays only about its own desires and concerns, it'll soon dry up. Instead, encourage prayers to include families, your greater church family, your community, and even the world. This is especially important when God doesn't seem to be answering readily or at all. But if you cultivate the attitude that "prayer together can change our world," new passion will erupt within your group.

2. Prayer isn't just the words

Instead, in a group situation, as one person gives voice to his or her thoughts, others pray along—adding an "amen" in their hearts to what's requested. Prayer isn't only speaking to God, but listening to him—waiting on his guidance, direction, and comfort.

3. Prayer comes alive when people see results

When God acts in response to prayer, people get excited. "Our prayers worked!" "God did it!" "Things are happening!" When people get the idea that God wants to work in the world on their behalf, they get energized and ready for more.

6 WAYS TO MAKE GROUP PRAYER MORE MEANINGFUL

How can you bring more fulfillment and meaning to the prayer life of your small group? Follow these suggestions.

1. Share answers before you start

Nothing kindles spiritual fire like knowing God is working in your midst. At the start of any small group prayer time, encourage those who've had answers to group prayer to talk about those answers with the group. This encourages others to believe that their prayers are worthwhile. It also assures them that future prayers can be answered just as surely and boldly.

2. Keep a prayer list

Simple as it is, many people don't do it. Urge your group members to make their own written lists of all prayers to keep in their wallets, pocketbooks, or personal organizers. When you get together in the small group, go through the lists and remind group members of items they may have forgotten.

3. Keep a group prayer journal

This is like the official prayer list record. Recruit one person to be the secretary. He or she records all the different things prayed about and then fills in the answers when they come. One way to do this is with index cards. Write the need or request at the top of the card along with the date. At each succeeding meeting, pass out the cards and continue in prayer about the concern until it's answered or God moves the person or situation in a different direction.

4. Follow up with each other

When you get together, ask questions about whether a specific prayer has been answered. Keep people motivated by reminding them of the prayers you've made and finding out when they're answered. Don't let people get by with a shrug. It's important to you, to your group, and to God that you all know what God is doing in your midst.

5. Pray big, pray little

Encourage people to realize that no prayer is too big or too little for God. Whether someone in the group needs a new house, direction on a new job, or guidance regarding major surgery, make it a matter of prayer. But don't forget the smaller things—like little aches and pains, problems of the day, affording a jacket for a child, or a special occasion you want to celebrate. Nothing is too big for God to deal with and nothing is too small for God to be concerned about. If it matters to you, it matters to God.

6. Celebrate answers to prayer

Remember to spend time praising God for the prayers he answers (which, in reality, is everything you pray about). Have an answered-prayer party. Gather group members together to tell about prayers they've seen answered during the last few months. Celebrate God's goodness and love in a tangible way.

8 THINGS YOUR SMALL GROUP CAN PRAY FOR

While your group will naturally spend time praying for your own needs as well as concerns about close friends and family members, don't limit your intercession to just those areas. Mix in these topics to bring freshness and energy to your small group prayer times.

1. Pastor and staff

Ask your pastor and ministry staff at your church to make your group aware of specific prayer requests they have. Let them know that you want to be a praying group, and you'll have no shortage of items for your prayer lists. Remember to follow up about God's answers for these requests.

2. The church directory

Bring in directories of your church members and encourage your group to pray for specific families by name. This is also a good reminder to pray for individuals and families who have visited your church, and for those whom God is leading to visit soon.

3. Missionaries

Request a list of all the missionaries your church supports. Compile information about them, their families, the country in which they serve, and any specific prayer requests they may have given to the church. Ask for copies of their support letters, which often contain prayer requests.

4. "Top Ten" list

Ask members of the group to create a list of ten unchurched individuals with whom they cross paths during the week. If some group members can't come up with a list of ten, ask God to bring into their lives additional people who need a personal relationship with Jesus. Pray over your lists, asking God to open doors and seeking his help in planting seeds in the lives of these people.

5. Newspaper or news magazine prayers

Bring in daily newspapers and weekly news magazines and have group members clip out items that your group can pray for. Have the group pray about the event, situation, need, or person by name. Spend time each week praying about current events.

6. Anything and everything in your world

Pray for specific countries. Mention them by name, even if you know nothing more about them. Pray for actors and others in the entertainment industry in Hollywood. Pray for the leaders and staffs of secular magazines and other news media. Pray for sports leaders and team members. Choose a particular segment of society (medical professionals, those in the judicial system, parents of school children, and so forth) and encourage the group to pray for them all that week. Build a list and pray for as many people as you can by name, even if you don't know specifics.

7. World day

Organize a special small group meeting to pray for different nations of the world. Use an almanac and ask group members to choose a specific nation that they'll research and pray about. Read facts about the country from the almanac and then pray for that nation as a group. You can also use a globe or world map to point out precisely where nations are located.

8. Influence

Take some time to brainstorm and list various influences in the world today. Pray about each of these as you see fit, asking God to do his will in circumstances that are sometimes too complex to understand. For example, you might pray about the advancing influence of Islam in the world and ask God to open doors for reaching out to these people with the message of the gospel.

12 PRACTICAL WAYS TO LIVE OUT WHAT YOU'VE LEARNED

If your small group meetings include a regular Bible study lesson, you may discover that you sometimes leave without ever really understanding how to apply what you've been studying. You'll indeed be an honored small group leader if you help your group make those connections.

Here are some activities that can be paired with a topical study, but many could become the focus of a whole meeting of your small group. After each of these activities, take time to rate the experience with these questions:

- On a scale of 1 (low) to 10 (high), how would you rank this experience for yourself?

- What was the most important insight you gained from this activity?

- How can you incorporate this quality into your life regularly?

1. Prayer

Have you ever heard of ACTS? Yes, Acts is a book in the New Testament that tells the story of the early church. But ACTS is also an acronym that can help your prayer time as a small group as well as in your personal prayer life. ACTS stands for the following:

Adoration of God;

Confession to God;

Thanksgiving for what God has done;

Supplication, asking humbly and earnestly, in accordance with God's will.

Write the letters ***A, C, T,*** and ***S*** across the top of a large piece of newsprint. As a group, brainstorm things to pray about that fall under these four categories. Then pray together, going through each category. Your group may want to revisit your piece of newsprint each week as a reminder to pray for all of the things they came up with.

2. One verse

Choose one verse of Scripture—perhaps a meaningful verse or short passage from your Bible study—that your group agrees to study and meditate on throughout the coming week. Study the verse, reflect on its meaning, and pray it to God. Try to focus on the verse several times a day. For example, think about the verse when you wake up, at work, as you eat lunch, as you exercise, and as you go to bed. When you meet again next week, be prepared to share what you've discovered.

3. Intense service

Place the names of all your small group members in a hat or bowl and draw names. You might want to consider having women draw women's names and men draw men's names. Have each person do at least one act of service per day for the person whose name he or she drew. At your next meeting, discuss what it was like to purposefully serve someone every day. How hard was it to remember? Was it difficult to think of something for each day? What insight does this give your group about serving others?

4. Meaningful worship

As a group, make plans to attend a worship service at a church that follows different worship traditions than your congregation does. If possible, arrange with leaders of the other church to attend and sit together as a group. Explain that your group is studying worship, and you want to learn from this sister congregation. Commit to one another to participate as fully as you can in the worship. You might even invite a group from the other church to return your visit at a later date. At your next meeting, talk about your experience together, particularly focusing on how a different approach to worship provides new meaning to your adoration of God.

5. One extra hour

As a group, commit that for the next week, you'll all surrender one hour daily that you'd typically spend watching television or reading a book, and that you'll spend that hour quietly with God each day. Take notes about what God is teaching you. Share what you learn from your extra time with God when you meet with your group next week.

6. Thanksgiving

Before members of your group head their separate ways this week, form groups of two or three, and have each pair or trio do one of the following to express thanks to God:

- write a poem
- write a song
- draw a picture
- create a skit

Have each pair or trio present its project to the rest of your group. Between presentations, encourage one another to thank God in silent or corporate prayer.

7. Listening to God

Spend the last thirty to sixty minutes of your meeting outdoors. If possible go to a park—one that isn't near traffic or crowded with people. Walk around the park, letting each member of the group wander wherever he or she likes. Listen carefully to the sounds around you. Notice the sounds that you're aware of immediately. Notice how much more you hear as time passes and you become more focused.

Try to focus all of your senses on one thing at a time:

- What do you see?
- What do you feel?
- What do you smell?

After spending ten or fifteen minutes becoming fully aware of your surroundings, turn your attention to God. Listen carefully to him. Use your senses to become aware of him. Be ready to tell your group what insights you gain.

8. Go team!

Plan a time together—perhaps your next regular meeting—where you'll play an active team game, such as softball, volleyball, touch football, basketball, or soccer. If some members of the group can't play physically active games, play a team board game such as Pictionary, Cranium, or Guesstures. Afterward, talk about the importance of each player on the team. Compare the team nature of the sport or game to the team nature of using spiritual gifts in the church.

9. Showers of encouragement

Before your small group disperses, take turns showering each other with words of encouragement. Sit in a circle and select someone as the "person to be encouraged." Have group members each say something encouraging to the person. The "encouraged" isn't allowed to speak or respond to any comments. After everyone has had an opportunity to share, select another person to be encouraged. Repeat the same process for everyone in the group.

10. Follow the leader

Go for a walk or a hike in unfamiliar territory. Take turns having each member of the group lead the hike, letting that person make the decisions that need to be made while leading. At your destination, discuss the following questions:

- What was it like to lead the group into unfamiliar territory?

- If you had to make a decision, what did that feel like and how did it affect the rest of the group?
- How did you feel when you weren't at the head of the pack?

11. Living out mercy

Instead of your regular small group meeting, go as a group to visit patients in a local hospice. Offer to sit with them, read to them, pray with them, or just listen. Bring small and cheery gifts, such as flowers. Or, ahead of time, have a children's Sunday school class make get-well cards for the patients. If your small group has musicians, find out if the facility would welcome a concert.

12. Joy party!

As a group, plan a celebration of joy—in other words, a party! Ask each group member to bring and share these things:
- a favorite joyful party food
- favorite joyful praise music
- at least five favorite clean jokes, funny stories, or cartoons

14 IDEAS FOR SMALL GROUP WORSHIP TIMES

Can you picture Jesus singing a hymn? Jesus lived a life of worship, honoring his Father with his words and actions, often going off by himself to pray (Mark 1:35, Luke 6:12). But sing? Yes, Jesus worshipped the Father in song as well. Here's how the Lord's Supper ended: "When they had sung a hymn, they went out to the Mount of Olives" (Matthew 26:30). Early Christians followed Jesus' lead and worshipped God in song. As the Apostle Paul said to Christians in Colosse, "Let the word of Christ dwell in you richly as you teach and admonish one another with all wisdom, and as you sing psalms, hymns and spiritual songs with gratitude in your hearts to God" (Colossians 3:16).

Why not set aside a segment of time to follow this tradition in your small group? How can you make the most of this opportunity? The following ideas will help your small group have vibrant praise and worship times.

1. Prayerfully select the right worship leader

The person you might think is the most natural to take the lead in this area may or may not be God's person for the position. Remember, God loves the praises of his people and is most interested in you achieving your goal of effective worship! He knows the people in your small group and each one's needs; he knows who he wants to build up and use in his service as a worship leader. So pray. Ask God to lead you to the right person, one not only with great musical abilities, but also with a heart of worship and the call of God.

2. It's about participation, not performance

While the worship leader will have a strong voice and sense of rhythm, it's important to remember that this isn't a performance, but participation singing. It's exalting the God of the universe together (Psalm 34:3). This is a key expectation you'll want to make clear upfront to the prospective worship leader. You'll know a worship leader is bordering on "performance" when the group is tempted to applaud his or her efforts rather than give God a "clap offering."

3. Study the significance of worship

The praise and worship segment of your small group isn't merely a time of corporate singing. It's turning your complete attention to God. It's not about people; it's all about God. It's focusing on who God is, what he's done, is doing, and what he promises to do. It's honoring, glorifying, and exalting God. It's two-way communication between mankind and the Creator. Don't let your small group miss the true meaning behind the hymns and choruses!

4. Yield to the Holy Spirit

Worship is more than just plopping down and singing along. Group members should all prayerfully prepare their hearts for worship. From song selection and preparation to leading and participating in small group worship, do it all with a heart that's yielded to God, open to him.

5. Plan the flow of worship

Use songs that relate to each other or that focus on the theme or topic of what your group is studying. Keep things simple—easy to play, easy to sing, no barriers to the experience of worship. Sing a variety of songs, not "the same ones we sing every week," and learn new songs from time to time.

6. Lead with or without instruments

The small group "instrument of choice" is the guitar, but a keyboard, CD or tape, or simply a cappella all can work fine. While they help with rhythm, instruments should never be the focus. Whatever "helps" you use, ensure that they enhance and don't detract from the time of worship.

7. Pay attention to openings and closings

How will the worship time begin? Will you read a particular verse, share a story, or simply grab a guitar and say, "Hey, let's circle up and sing a few songs"? And how will you conclude this time together? The leader may simply "drop out" accompaniment on the last verse with the group singing it a cappella, then give a nod to the small group leader. Or you may wish to end with a prayer or a call to silence, for example, to ponder a particular matter of the heart. A good worship leader will make it a habit to thank the group for their participation.

8. Create an atmosphere where it's OK for everyone to sing

Make sure everyone has or can see the words. Remind them that the Bible only calls us to "make a joyful noise," not even necessarily a good one! If appropriate, have the group stand in a circle. Then again, allow participants to stay in the background, "out of the circle," if they prefer. God may be dealing with them in ways you can't imagine, so create an environment that allows the Holy Spirit to work.

9. Know the songs by heart

The leader's goal is to remove any barrier to what God wants to do in your worship time. Consider memorizing each song's words and music. When you have to focus too much on a piece of paper for words and/or music, you won't be able to look people in the eye or get the most accurate sense of what God is doing among the group.

10. Allow for personal sharing

You may wish to lead into a song with an appropriate Scripture verse—perhaps a psalm—related to the words of the song, or encourage a member of the group to do so. If appropriate and as time permits, share (or encourage others to do so) something that punctuates the premise of the song. For example, related to the song "God Is Good All the Time," ask, "How has God been good to you this week?"

11. Allow for individual expression

Some group members will raise their hands as an expression of reaching out to and receiving from the Lord. Others aren't comfortable doing that. Some will sing loudly, others will sing quietly. Some will keep their eyes open, while others will have them closed in prayer. Be sensitive to how the Holy Spirit is moving in your midst, and seek to be a tool in his hands to enhance what God is doing.

12. Write original music

Sometimes God gives small group worship leaders (perhaps in partnership with small group leaders) a vision to create original music. If the Lord is really using a song or songs you've written, consider introducing your original music to the person who heads up worship music at your church, and/or sending it to a publisher. Such music is an affirmation that the Lord is in your midst and extending his blessing. God can use something birthed out of an authentic worship experience to have an incredible impact for eternity's sake around the world!

13. Be alert for spiritual attack

When you desire to live a life that honors and glorifies God and to help others do the same through praise and worship, expect spiritual attacks. The enemy is a roaring lion on the prowl for someone to tear apart (1 Peter 5:8). Pray for God to clothe you with his full armor (Ephesians 6:10-18).

14. Remain teachable

There are a variety of ways you can stay on top of new worship music and practical helps produced by and available to worship leaders. For example, check out these Web sites:

- www.worshipideas.com. Free membership gives you access to a weekly newsletter with "tips on building an effective contemporary worship ministry," and much more.

- www.songs4worship.com. A one-stop online worship resource with all the latest in praise and worship, plus links to browse music, other resources, music news and views, ministry and leadership, and worship life.

- www.worshipmusic.com. The mission of this site is "to increase worship on the earth!" It includes a store for worship and praise music, with titles from Vineyard, Integrity, Hosanna, Maranatha, Worship Together, Hillsongs, and Brentwood, along with "the largest collection of quality independent label worship music."

15 WAYS TO MAKE COMMUNION MORE MEANINGFUL

While some leaders might not even think about celebrating the rite of the Lord's Supper with their small groups, it's exciting to think that Jesus celebrated the first communion with his twelve disciples—a group about the size of an average small group! Should small groups celebrate this sacrament?

Communion is meant to be a time of reflection and remembrance—reflecting on your sins and confessing them; and remembering all that the Lord has done for you. Certainly, there's something very right about celebrating the rite of communion with a group of people who are getting to know you well, who love you, and who care about you.

With these thoughts in mind, here are some ways to make communion more meaningful for your small group.

1. Integrate music

Your group's time of communion can be accompanied by a CD or tape of recorded music. Select music that fosters reflection and reverence. After each song, introduce a different element of the communion time. This can last through several songs, and participants can sing along if they desire.

2. Remember Jesus

As you lay the groundwork for communion, group members choose favorite stories about Jesus and retell them or read them from the Bible. This focuses everyone on Jesus' life and sacrifice.

3. Include a time of confession

In 1 Corinthians 11:28, Paul admonishes us to look within and examine ourselves. Often, opening up the communion to an outward, verbal confession of sin makes it more meaningful. This becomes a time to look back to Jesus' death on the cross for forgiveness, and also to look forward to his coming and our reunion with him forever.

4. Incorporate various readings

Give each member of your group a passage of Scripture to read as the communion elements are passed. Select passages that stir a look at one's life, as well as promises of God and thoughts about his attributes. Group members can also select passages spontaneously, simply choosing favorites or picking passages that follow a specific theme (such as confession, worship, love, goodness, and so on).

5. Teach about the elements

The small group leader brings out the qualities of these two parts of communion. Because unleavened bread contains no yeast, it is completely dead and lifeless. Wine, on the other hand, is filled with good bacteria. These two elements represent both the death and life of Jesus himself. Accenting these truths can enhance the group's participation in communion and illustrate the depth of God's work.

6. Learn the traditions of Passover and communion

Invite a local rabbi to your group to demonstrate how the Passover Seder took place. You can then tell how Jesus used the same elements to initiate communion. This will not only instruct the group but will build friendships with people outside the faith.

7. List answered prayers

Consider creating a "Book of Remembrance" so that at each communion small group members can talk about how God has answered prayers, remembering Jesus' faithfulness. Recruit someone to be in charge of keeping the book and adding to it each time your group celebrates communion.

8. Dress up

Most of us think of communion as a very serious and reflective time, but that doesn't mean you can't be creative. Ask group members to dress up as disciples and come to a Lord's Supper evening. During the evening, after celebrating communion, group members try to guess who each participant is dressed as. Costumes might include clues, such as Peter with a fishing net thrown over his shoulder or Matthew carrying a tax ledger.

9. Examine communion through the ages

Do some research and briefly talk about different ways communion has been celebrated in different times.

10. Add a mission focus

Is a missionary visiting your church? Invite him or her to your small group and ask how communion is conducted in the country where he or she serves. Your group can then spend time praying for the missionary's work in detail.

11. Focus on devotion

Ask each member of the group to bring a favorite reading from a contemporary or classic book written about Jesus or about devotion to him. Group members read their selections and lead brief discussions around the communion setting.

12. Craft a chalice

Provide clay for people to use to fashion a chalice. Each group member can use clay that dries to create a symbolic chalice. Or if you have access to a kiln, you can use ceramic clay, fire it, and then use the vessels at the group's next communion service.

13. Bake bread

Ask each member to bring a recipe and ingredients to bake bread to use in the communion service (they can check local libraries or do an Internet search). Based on your tradition, you make the call on whether the bread needs to be unleavened, but you'll be surprised at how many different recipes do exist that qualify as unleavened.

14. Explore other traditions

Invite a priest from the Catholic church (to explain the concept of transubstantiation), a minister from a Lutheran church (to explain consubstantiation), and someone from a tradition that regards communion as a remembrance. Discuss the various thoughts. This will accent the depth of Christian traditions and offer poignant reasons why you celebrate communion the way you do. (An alternative is for the leader or a group member to research these traditions and meanings, and to present a brief explanation of each.)

15. Like it was back then

Celebrate communion the same way Jesus did with his disciples, reclining about a table and as part of a meal. Your group might combine this with idea 8 ("Dress up").

Endnote

1. Marlene LeFever, *Learning Styles* (Colorado Springs, CO: David C. Cook Publishing Co., 2002), 20-21.

GREAT ESCAPES
*When Your Group Needs to Depart
From the Ordinary*

Great Escapes—
When Your Group Needs to Depart From the Ordinary

Sometimes, the normal and everyday feels good—secure and reassuring. But sometimes the normal and everyday feels boring—like you're stuck in a rut or running on one of those little wheels in a hamster cage.

It can help energize you and your group to do something just out of the ordinary. This section offers some ways to escape your routine and grow spiritually at the same time.

5 READY-TO-GO SPECIAL OCCASION BIBLE STUDIES

While you can probably find or come up with Bible study material for the typical Christian holidays, such as Christmas or Easter, you might struggle to find material for other special occasions—such as the birth of a baby, an upcoming vacation, or a farewell to a group member who's moving away. These ready-to-go studies provide a way to commemorate and bring meaning to these occasions during your small group's study time.

Baby Blessings: Quivering With Joy

When to use this study: When a couple in your group gives birth or adopts a baby.

Icebreaker: If you have a real bow and arrows, set up a target in your backyard (or a garage or basement if you're not concerned about damage). Or you can forego the target and let each person see how far he or she can shoot the arrow with the bow.

If you don't have a bow and arrow available—and this is certainly a safer option—purchase a child's bow and arrow set and let group members take turns to see how far they can shoot the arrow.

Following this activity, discuss these questions:

• In what way are our children like arrows?

• As parents, what target are we shooting them toward?

Bible connect: Psalm 127:3-5.
Optional: Psalm 139:13-16.

Priming the pump: We live in a culture that tries in some ways to diminish the importance of family. In a world of child abuse, abortion, and broken families, it's easy to have a cynical view of children—even for Christians who have kids. The world seems to tell us to flee from anything that impedes our freedom and doesn't bring us joy. And let's face it, raising kids is tough!

Scripture reminds us that children are a blessing—even a "reward." In the past, people didn't need to be reminded of this. Yes, having more children meant more mouths to feed, but it also meant that a family had more potential for wealth and growth. This was a somewhat practical matter: if you made your living by raising crops, you could raise a lot more crops if you had more help. Some families were almost like mini corporations with self-raised employees! With

SECTION 6: Great Escapes

⑥

more help, a farmer, rancher, or dairy herdsman could expand. More family members also meant more protection and more of a voice in society.

One pastor used Psalm 127:3-5 to liken children to arrows that parents shoot out into society. By sending out Christlike children into the world, a family expands its influence. So instead of just two people—husband and wife—living for Christ, a whole family is spreading the gospel. The idea of growing workers for the kingdom isn't a concept we think about often. But it's an interesting idea to ponder.

Discussion questions

Note: If you have a large group, to encourage maximum participation, break into smaller groups to discuss these questions.

- If someone told you people should not have children because the world is too evil, or the world is too crowded, how would you respond?

- Beyond populating the earth, what's the purpose of having children?

- Why do you think God created the model of family?

- How can the family be a vehicle of evangelism?

- How did you feel the first time you saw each of your children?

- In what ways are children a blessing? How do the blessings balance with the challenge and heartaches?

In action: Have an autograph book in the classroom. This can be a journal or a simple notebook (anything with blank pages). Pass it around and ask each person to write down one tip for the new parents.

Optional: Encourage parents to thank God for their children this week by telling their children what they love about them. If the kids are old enough to read, encourage parents to write a note to the children telling them how special they are.

Moving On

When to use this study: When a group member is moving away.

Icebreaker: Create a treasure hunt. Break your group into teams, give clues, and let teams try to find a hidden item. In fitting with the theme of moving, the item might be a child's pair of shoes, an old suitcase, or something else to indicate being on the go.

Following this activity, discuss these questions:
- In a move, what are things that are "lost" or feel lost?
- What emotion do you tend to associate with moving?

Bible connect: Genesis 12:1-5.
Optional: Exodus 13:21-22; Proverbs 3:5-6; Jeremiah 29:11; and Romans 8:35, 37-39.

Priming the pump: When God told Abram to move, he didn't tell him exactly where to go. He simply said, "Go to the land I will show you" (Genesis 12:1).

While we often have a little more guidance than that when we move, it can be difficult to uproot. Even when the move is for a great reason—a terrific job or moving closer to loved ones—it can still be difficult. In fact, even when change is good, it still creates a significant amount of stress.

Although moving means a phase of life is ending, it also means that a new chapter of life is just beginning. When we move, we'll meet new people, find new friends, learn new lessons, and face situations where we'll experience God's mercy and grace and learn from him.

As our group prepares to say goodbye to one of our own—someone we have loved and cared for—we want to remind you that God goes before you. Just as God went before the Israelites as they traveled to the Promised Land, God leads us—even when we don't exactly know what our final destination will be. A move is a new chapter, filled with hope.

And while we may not have daily interaction with you, we're still praying for you and we'll always be a part of your life—and you'll always be a part of ours.

Discussion questions

Note: If you have a large group, to encourage maximum participation, break into smaller groups to discuss these questions.

- How many times have you moved from one town to another?
- What do you feel is the hardest thing about moving?
- Why is moving difficult?
- What are some good things about moving?
- How can God use a move in our lives?
- How can a move affect our relationship with God?
- What tips do you have for the person who's moving?

In action: Create a blessings book for the group member who is moving. Encourage each person in the group to write a blessing for the person leaving. Pray over the person, thanking God for this individual's life and asking God to bless him or her in the move, the new life, and new responsibilities. Ask God to guide the person to the right church and to people who will be sources of encouragement.

Optional: Make a "We Love You" video for the people leaving (you can make this after they've left and send it to them as a housewarming gift). Encourage people to share encouragement from Scripture on this video, and to answer the question, "What does [name] mean to me?" This can be as simple as just setting up a camera before and after the small group meeting. Or if you have a video buff in your group, let him or her be creative.

⑥ SECTION 6: Great Escapes

Vacation: You Deserve a Break

When to use this study: When a group member, couple, or family is headed on vacation; at the beginning of the summer season when many people will likely be going on vacation.

Icebreaker: Ask group members to take a slip of paper (sticky notes work well also) and write on it three places they've gone to for a vacation. Put all the slips of paper in a basket or other container. Draw one, read the three places, and have the group guess who the note refers to.

Following this activity, discuss these questions:
- What is your "dream" vacation and why?
- How do you typically feel right before, during (in the middle of), and immediately after a vacation?

Bible connect: Mark 6:30-32.
Optional: Matthew 11:28-29.

Priming the pump: Vacations can be very valuable for providing a time of rest, refreshment, and a needed change of pace.

In Mark 6:30-32, the disciples had been busy. At the beginning of the chapter, they were sent out to preach and teach in Christ's name. During this time, John had been beheaded and now the disciples were gathered around Jesus again. Still, people clamored for more. Jesus finally told them, "Come with me by yourselves to a quiet place and get some rest" (Mark 6:34).

We all need to get away once in a while for a rest. A change of scenery, routine, and people do most of us a world of good. In fact, God instituted rest from the very beginning, resting on the seventh day of creation (Genesis 2:2), and later directing that we shouldn't work on the Sabbath (Exodus 20:10). In the New Testament, Jesus tells us that "The Sabbath was made for man, not man for the Sabbath" (Mark 2:27).

Nothing is wrong with getting away and taking some time to rest and relax. Nothing's wrong with taking some time to have fun. Wherever we go, God goes with us.

Discussion questions

Note: If you have a large group, to encourage maximum participation, break into smaller groups to discuss these questions.

• What has been your most memorable vacation and what made it so?

• What should be the focus of a vacation?

• How can we remember to focus on rest and fun during vacation and not let it get too hectic?

• How does being away from home help refresh us mentally?

• How can we use a vacation time as a time to grow closer to God?

• In what ways can a vacation be challenging to us in our relationship with God?

In action: Discuss different group members' plans for vacation. As a group, take turns praying that God will bless and protect you on your journeys.

Optional: At the end of the summer, have a small group vacation party. Encourage group members to bring pictures and souvenirs and to tell about their vacations.

Grandparent's Day

When to use this study: Grandparent's Day is the first Sunday after Labor Day. You could also use this study when group members become grandparents for the first (or twentieth) time.

Leader note: As you walk and talk through this study, gently encourage grandparents to invest in their grandchildren's lives. Help them see this as a ministry with eternal rewards. If a group member or couple are empty nesters but don't have grandchildren yet, or they do but their grandchildren live a long distance away, perhaps they can become surrogate grandparents to some children in your church—even those of other group members. For grandparents who can't be with their grandchildren, emphasize the power of prayer (and letting their grandkids know they're praying for them).

Icebreaker: Ask anyone who has at least one grandchild to stand. Tell them to remain standing if they have two; then to remain standing if they have three grandchildren. Keep going until only one person (or one couple) is standing.

Celebrate every grandparent in the group by giving them each some time to brag about and show pictures of their grandkids.

Then discuss these questions:

• When you think of your grandparents, what comes to mind?

• What is something you learned from a grandparent?

Bible connect: Deuteronomy 4:9-10.
Optional: Proverbs 13:22, 17:6; and 2 Timothy 1:5.

⑥ SECTION 6: Great Escapes

Priming the pump: Many people who are looking for ministry in life don't need to look any further than their own offspring's home! Parents are frazzled today. In many homes, both Mom and Dad work, and they never have as much time for their kids as they'd like. They want to teach faith principles and instill a strong faith in their children. Exhausted by the demands of life, they can use a backup—someone to provide help and teaching and love.

Grandparents can play a wonderful role with their grandchildren. What grandparents instill in their grandkids' lives will last way beyond their own time—into future generations.

In our culture, of course, grandparents are also busier than ever. Unfortunately, some won't commit time to their grandkids, saying instead, "I've done my time." It takes a real selflessness and a love commitment for grandparents to choose to be there for their grandchildren.

Discussion questions

Note: If you have a large group, to encourage maximum participation, break into smaller groups to discuss these questions.

- What are some ways grandparents can pour themselves into their grandchildren?

- What are the sacrifices grandparents sometimes have to make to spend time with their grandkids?

- What are the best ways parents can invest in their children's children?

- How can grandparents teach grandchildren about faith? What are some practical things they can do?

- What kind of faith and/or family traditions have been a part of your life? Why are these traditions important? What kind of traditions can you create with your grandchildren (or your children)?

- What can grandparents do to strengthen bonds when they live far from grandchildren?

- How can grandparents pray effectively for their grandchildren?

In action: Ask each grandparent to list actions he or she can take to minister to grandkids. Invite grandparents in the group to put a star by one thing they can do during the coming week. Encourage them to do one thing each week to help build a relationship with their grandchildren.

Ask parents and others in the group (nongrandparents) to list how they'd like to see their parents and other senior adults in the church be involved in the faith aspects of their children's (or future children's) lives.

Optional: Hang a large whiteboard on the wall. Let grandparents list their grandchildren on this. Or have grandparents list their grandchildren's names on sheets of paper and then put all the pieces of paper into a basket. Using the wall of names or basket of names as a reference, and asking volunteers from the group to pray out loud, commit these children to the Lord. Then pray a prayer of dedication for the grandparents in your group to be missionaries to their grandchildren.

■ ■ ■

When Death Strikes: Responding With Pain and Celebration

When to use this study: After someone in the group has had a family member or close friend pass away; when someone from your group has died.

Leader note: Different people grieve in different ways. You might have heard of Elisabeth Kubler-Ross's theory on the stages of grief. Some people will go through the typical stages of anger, anguish, questioning, depression, acceptance, and so on. But others will go through different stages, and they'll go through stages at different times. They'll grieve in different ways, according to their personalities. Some will be furious at God, while others will never feel that anger. And grief is cyclical. A person may go through the emotions of grief, move on, and then perhaps go through that same stage again with more or less intensity. A great resource is *When Your People Are Grieving,* by Harold Ivan Smith (Kansas City, MO: Beacon Hill Press, 2001).

Be sure to have patience with members of your group if they act out of character for a while. Realize that simply talking about death will bring up a lot of questions that you might not have answers for. One good response is, "I don't know exactly why life works this way, but I do know that God feels our pain and understands our grief."

Also try to bring out the celebration of a person's life. We're so distraught the person is gone from us, but if they knew Jesus as Savior, you can celebrate that they're now whole and in the presence of God.

If you're going to tackle the subject of death with your group, try not to worry about doing things right or wrong or saying something right or wrong. Just express love and give people a place to talk. Have plenty of tissues handy. Listen, cry with them, offer an appropriate hug or squeeze, and pray with and for them.

Icebreaker: Instead of an icebreaker for this lesson, spend extra time in discussion. People in grief need to talk. Start the conversation with these questions:

- How did the news of [name's] death affect you?
- When was the first time death touched your life, and how did you respond?

Bible connect: John 11:32-45

Priming the pump: It's OK to grieve. "Jesus wept" (John 11: 35) when he went to see Mary and Martha following the death of Lazarus. Jesus knew he was going to raise Lazarus. But still he cried—validating the grief and pain we feel when someone we love dies.

Discussion questions

- Why do you think Jesus cried at the funeral of Lazarus?

- How do you think people responded when Lazarus arose?

- What are ways a funeral can be a celebration?

- What comes to mind when you think of [name]? How did he or she make a difference in your life?

- What can we do to minister to those left behind? What can we do for [name's] spouse and/or children?

In action: Have a card or cards that people can sign, expressing grief to the loved ones of the person who has died. Encourage group members to do more than sign a name; instead, they should use this opportunity to tell the surviving family members what this person meant in their lives.

If your group comes up with ideas on ways to serve the family, assign the ideas so people will follow through.

Also, as you talk about what the deceased person meant in your lives, you could tape the conversation. Give the recording to the person's loved ones. Hearing how he or she ministered to others will help them. You might even set up an "audio card." Instead of members signing a note, they can speak into the microphone their condolences for the remaining family, and mention why they loved this person.

Pray together for the person's family.

Optional: If the person who died was a Christian and your group is going to be in tears anyway, you might play the Ray Boltz song, "Thank You."

2 ONE-DAY RETREATS FOR SMALL GROUPS

It's no secret—time alone with God can revitalize, renew, and empower us. Extended time alone with God provides a perspective on life that isn't easily captured in our daily devotion times. Moving away from the familiar—to be alone and quiet before God—gives us a vantage point that can't be beaten.

Personal getaways with God often happened in high places. Jesus, while walking this earth, was routinely energized by time spent alone with his Father in the hills surrounding Jerusalem. You can extend the blessings of personal mountaintop encounters with God to the members of your group by organizing a one-day retreat designed to introduce them to extended time alone with the Lord.

God meets with people wherever they are—whether on the top of a mountain, walking along a road, or in the belly of a great big fish. Amazing things can happen when we're alone in God's presence. Meeting with God is about getting away from things that distract us. Group retreats have been popular for years. Now personal retreats are on the rise. A one-day retreat is a structured way for your small group to accomplish both—to get to know each other better and learn more about God during some study and devotional times together; and also to get to know God better and learn more about yourselves during extended quiet times.

The basic agenda for a one-day retreat looks like this:

Thirty minutes: Opening devotion

Two to three hours: Extended quiet time

One hour: Small group Bible study

Thirty minutes: Closing devotion

You can also add time for meals, recreation, and/or service projects. Here's one possible schedule on a Sunday:

9:00	Attend worship service and Bible class.
11:30	Depart (lunch on the road).
1:30	Arrive at retreat site.
1:45	Opening devotion.*
2:15	Extended quiet time.*
4:30	Small group Bible study.*
5:30	Dinner.
6:30	Closing devotion.*
7:00	Depart for home.

*Content for these component parts is provided on the pages that follow.

To whet your group's appetite for mountain air, consider reading the following stories together at one of your weekly meetings prior to your retreat. Ask, "What did each person receive as a result of this mountaintop experience with God?"

- Exodus 3:1-12—the story of Moses and the burning bush
- 1 Kings 19:1-18—the story of Elijah's restoration on Mount Horeb
- Matthew 17:1-8—the story of Jesus' transfiguration

Don't plan this event by yourself. Ask each person in your group to help. Group members can help find a location, deal with finances, lead parts of the retreat (opening, closing, music, devotions, and Bible study), and coordinate meals and transportation.

A few weeks before your group's retreat, read through all the material and make copies of the pages you will need (pages 174-184 for Retreat 1 and pages 185-193 for Retreat 2).

In addition, make copies of the pages each person will need (the Retreat Packet Material—pages 177-181 for Retreat 1 and pages 187-190 for Retreat 2).

At one of your regular small group meetings, at least a week prior to your retreat, place the name of each group member on a separate piece of paper. Put these slips of paper in a hat or bowl and pass the hat or bowl around the group for each group member to draw a name. Encourage group members to specifically and intentionally pray for the person whose name they drew. Ask the Lord to use this retreat to reveal himself in new ways, to renew in each individual a passion for his kingdom, to restore and heal the wounded and weary places of your hearts, and to empower and equip you for the specific call he has for your lives.

The Hands of God

General retreat supplies needed:

- things necessary for worship music (instruments, song sheets, and so forth)
- whiteboard/markers, blackboard/chalk, or newsprint or flip-chart paper and markers
- retreat packets (copies of pages 177-181)—one per person, to be handed out after the opening devotion
- Also see the supplies lists for the opening devotion (below) and the small group Bible study (page 182).

Note: Every group member should plan to bring the following items to the retreat:

- a Bible
- a pen or pencil
- a notebook, some paper, or a journal

Opening Devotion—Hands in Action

Supplies needed:

For every three people in your small group you will need:

- a roll of masking tape
- a button-down shirt
- a shoe with laces
- a pen and piece of paper

Divide your small group members into subgroups of three. The trios can pull together chairs and sit in small circles. Pass out the masking tape. The person in each group whose name is closest to the letter *A* must secure the thumbs on both hands down into the palms of his or her hands. Immobilize each thumb with tape. Others in the group will probably have to lend a helping hand.

The person to the right needs to hold up his or her index fingers, as if saying, "I'm number 1" with both hands. Using the tape, immobilize the other four digits, leaving the index finger free.

The final person in the group should tape down his or her thumbs and first two fingers with tape, leaving the pinky and ring fingers free on both hands.

Now pass out the remaining items (the shirt, the shoe, the pen and paper) to each group—one to each person.

Explain that you'll be rotating through the trios, with each person having sixty seconds to button as many buttons as possible on the shirt, tie the shoe, or write his or her name and address using the pen and paper. Call out "Go" and time the groups for sixty seconds, calling out the time at fifteen-second intervals. After one minute, move the items to the right and time the groups for another sixty seconds. Repeat one last time for the trio members to work with their final items.

Now ask each trio to discuss these questions (you may want to write these down somewhere that everyone can see):

- What was the most challenging activity for you?

- Which one was the easiest?

- Imagine living your life this way. What other activities would be challenging? impossible? easy?

After the questions have been discussed, share the following thoughts in your own words:

Our hands are amazing! They testify to God's creative ingenuity. If we had to live the rest of our lives with our hands immobilized as they are now, our hands would frustrate and fail us regularly.

Even fully functioning hands don't always work the wonders we desire. They blunder—causing breaks and spills. They may not write as neatly as we would like. They may not type as quickly as we desire.

They may have never completed a successful free throw. Let's face it. Our hands fail us. So do the hands of others.

In the entire world there is only one set of hands that will never fail us. Whether it's in the arena of provision, protection, guidance, or salvation, the hands of God work daily miracles for us.

Let's pray. (Offer an opening prayer.)

Extended Quiet Time

Following the opening devotion, you are just about ready to send your group out for this portion of the retreat. Before group members head off on their own, cover the following:

- If you haven't already, distribute retreat packets (copies of pages 177-181) to everyone in the group.

- Share directions and/or maps of places to go for complete solitude, as well as a map of hiking trails, if available.

- If your group is confined to a single, large room, consider playing soft instrumental CDs to provide some background music. Prepare a refreshment table of drinks and snacks if you desire.

- Explain to your group that the extended quiet time is divided into six sections: God's Invitation, My Expectation, Adoration, Meditation, Supplication, and Celebration. Each section has a Scripture focus, along with a question or two to reflect on or a suggested activity—except for the section titled Meditation. The Meditation section invites us to peek into the heart of God as we reflect on the tenderness and power of his mighty hands. The goal isn't to complete this section, but to gladly receive what he longs to give us through the promises and truth of his Word.

In your own words, say: "It's time to head our separate ways. The first thing you'll find in your retreat material is a letter. Take the time to read it. It will set the stage and allow you to embrace all that God has waiting for you."

6

SECTION 6: Great Escapes

Retreat Packet Material

Dear friend in Christ,

Welcome! Welcome to this quiet place. An unhurried, quiet afternoon isn't a regular occurrence for most of us. It may feel a bit strange, yet we're in good company. For centuries, when God's people were off alone, away from the familiar, everyday things of life, God had a way of making himself known in remarkable ways. God is the same today. With great care, he'll orchestrate these quiet hours to prepare your heart for all he has in store for you.

But first, it's important to relax and unwind. This isn't a race. You don't have to do anything. The goal of the next two hours is to simply enjoy being in God's presence.

If you're like most people, you're underrested and overstressed. One of God's gifts for you in the next few hours is rest. So do what you need to do to slow down. Focus on each minute, each hour. Take deep breaths. Take a walk. Listen for birds. Enjoy a cup of tea. Lie in the grass and watch the clouds. Wiggle your toes in the sand. Skip some stones. Follow an ant. Catch a frog. You are free to be, to rest, and to enjoy two hours of no expectations!

When you're feeling rested and ready, turn your attention to God. Invite him to come near, asking him to make you fully receptive to the Holy Spirit's leading.

Go where he leads. Dig into the retreat material. Read your favorite psalm. Reflect. Journal. Pray. Sing. Rest some more. You can use this guided retreat resource, but do so only if it helps you draw near to the throne of grace. Be still or move around—whatever helps you sense the closeness of God.

Welcome to this time alone with the Lord.

Retreat Packet 1 • Page 1

God's Invitation

Meditate on Matthew 11:28-30. What three words in these verses are most captivating? How are they speaking to you today?

My Expectation

Carefully read Psalm 63:1-5. Consider writing a letter to God, expressing all that fills your heart today—the joys and the challenges.

Adoration

Meditate on Psalm 5:7. Spend time doing whatever you need to do to bow before the Lord in praise and adoration.

Meditation

Read Romans 15:4 to prepare your heart to focus on power of God's Word.

As you read on, you'll find four scriptural reflections on the "Hands of God." For this time of meditation, you can use as many or as few of these reflections as you desire.

Reflection 1: *God's Creative Handiwork*

As we acknowledge the handiwork of God in creation, we stand in awe at the display of his unimaginable power to "speak" things into existence (Genesis 1:3). In our Creator, however, we also see the masterful dedication and expertise of one who works with his hands (Job 10:8-9). The hands of God display the genius of his power to create, form, and sustain all things visible and unseen.

Pause, Praise, Ponder, and Pray

Read Psalm 19:1-4; 95:1-7; and Isaiah 64:8.

- Reflect on three things that leave you in awe of God's majestic creativity.

Retreat Packet 1 • Page 2

• What do those things reveal about their Creator?

Reflection 2: *God's Strong Hands*

Strength is the source of comfort. Where we're weak, God is strong. Where we're strong, our God is stronger still. Always—the one who goes before us, beside us, and behind us possesses unfathomable power, strength, and might. We're in good hands.

Pause, Praise, Ponder, and Pray

Reflect on the words of 2 Samuel 22:17-20 and Isaiah 41:9-10, 13.

• What promises do these verses contain for seasons wrought with overwhelming challenges?

• What one thing does God ask of us?

• Why does he choose to be our Redeemer?

Reflection 3: *The Heavy Hand of God*

We've all felt it—that heaviness of heart when our soul is burdened by what we've done or left undone. The weight is relentless. The relief—found first at the foot of the cross and then at the empty tomb—surrounds us with songs of deliverance.

Pause, Praise, Ponder, and Pray

Read Psalm 32 (focus on verses 1-5).

• What is making your heart heavy?

• When you are weighed down, where do you turn?

Turn. Run! God will meet you more than halfway, because he's running faster than you can imagine and his arms are opened wide (Luke 15:20).

Retreat Packet 1 • Page 3

Reflection 4: *The Hand of God Provides*

From potatoes to petunias, porcupines to people, our Lord God provides for all of creation. He promises provision throughout each season of our lives. When hearts are parched and bodies are depleted, we're reminded to look to the one who holds all the treasuries of heaven in the palm of his hand. In his time and in his way, he'll provide.

Pause, Praise, Ponder, and Pray

Read Psalm 145 and Isaiah 41:17-20.

• Make a list of God's provision from the psalm (verses 7, 15-16, 19).

• Which of these things would you like to specifically talk to God about today?

• Recount ten acts of the Lord's goodness and provision in your life.

• Reread Psalm 145:1-7. Reflect on the verbs: *exalt, praise, commend, tell, speak, meditate, proclaim, celebrate,* and *joyfully sing*. Allow your adoration to well up and overflow.

Supplication

As you near the end of your extended quiet time, slowly read the words of Psalm 116:1-2.

God longs for us to come to him with specifics. This breeds intimacy in your relationship with God. Lay your heart's desires before the Lord, trusting him to hear and respond as a loving Father. Pray, but don't neglect to quiet your heart and listen in response.

Pray for

• your family and friends, their burdens and cares

- your small group and the ministries of your church
- those you know who don't yet have a relationship with the Lord
- yourself
- your own burdens
- your dreams and desires
- your hunger for the presence of God

Celebration

Read Psalms 8:9–9:2.

Thank God for meeting with you in this place. Make a list of what he's revealing to you, what you're experiencing, and what insights you're gleaning from his Word.

When finished, gather back together with the group at the designated time and place.

Small Group Bible Study

> **Supplies needed:**
> • sheets of paper (regular or construction)—one per person
> • markers

Open with prayer.

Share the questions listed below with your group (you may want to post these on a board or make copies to distribute). Ask each person to select one or two of the questions to respond to, sharing his or her thoughts with the group.

- What did you learn about yourself today?
- What did you learn about God?
- How did he make himself known to you?
- How did you experience stillness today?
- What was most challenging?
- What aspect of this day was difficult?
- How did you experience the power of God?

Read Exodus 40:36-38. In your own words, share the following thoughts:

"There's a road stretched out before us. What's yours like? Is it steep? narrow? wide and bumpy? barren? dark and dangerous? level—but full of hairpin curves? Draw a picture of the road you travel."

Once group members have finished drawing their roads, ask them to share the drawings and brief explanations of them with the group.

Read Psalm 37:23-24. Ask the group:

- Has God's hand been obvious or subtle during this leg of your journey? What emotions do these verses evoke?

Read Psalm 139:23-24. To provide a prayer focus for the close of this small group time, share your thoughts on one or both of these questions:

- As God was searching your heart today, what did he reveal to you?

- How has God used this retreat to provide a guiding light to lead you in the way of righteousness?

Close by praying for each other in whatever way your group is accustomed to praying.

Before dismissing for dinner, collect the "roadway" drawings, as these will be used again during the closing devotion.

Closing Devotion

Plan a closing (using the suggested agenda that follows) that allows participants to come down from the mountain with a peaceful heart. Encourage each other to share your favorite verses about God's peace, provision, and protection. Worship the Lord with grateful hearts.

Agenda:

- Offer an opening prayer.
- Sing worship songs together.
- Read the devotional story "Hand in Hand" (on the next page).
- Read Psalm 139:5-12.
- Pass out the roadway drawings and have each person trace his or hand over their road drawings.
- Ask the group to share their favorite verse or passage on peace, provision, and God's protection.
- Sing more worship songs.
- Close in prayer (form a prayer circle and hold hands).

Hand in Hand

A four-year-old boy named Sam and his mom were enjoying a trip to a local children's museum. A new exhibit had opened and Sam could barely contain his excitement. Upon entering, they saw a small doorway leading to a dark tunnel. They had no idea what they would encounter, but Sam seemed up to the challenge. Side by side and hand in hand (not an easy feat while crawling on all fours) they entered the blackness. Sam instantly drew back and became hesitant—surprised by his complete inability to see.

"Mommy, I don't like this!"

"It's really dark inside, isn't it? It's a tunnel and it will lead us through a maze to a door on the other side. It's going to be very dark and we won't be able to see, but if you want to go, I'll be right here. I'll hold your hand the whole time."

He sat and thought for a minute. Every ounce of him wanted to attempt this new adventure, but fear battered his heart. Eventually, the adventurous side of Sam won, and inch-by-inch he and his mom crept inside.

Everything was going just fine, when, without any display of mounting fear, Sam let out an anguished sob followed by a steady stream of loud, wailing cries. The darkness had overwhelmed him.

"Sam, listen to me...I know you can't see Mommy, but I'm right here! Do you feel my hand? This is my hand! I'm right here."

Instantly, there was calm and quietness. In an unbelievably chipper voice he replied, "Oh, Mommy! I forgot I was holding your hand."

With confidence and courage, this little adventurer—hand resting securely in the grip of Mom's tender care—crawled on through the dark tunnel until they reached the very end. Once outside in the wonderful light, they celebrated with hugs and a round of high fives.

Listen to the one whose hands hold us now.

■ ■ ■

Quiet Waters and Living Streams

> **General retreat supplies needed:**
>
> - things necessary for worship music (instruments, song sheets, and so forth)
> - whiteboard/markers, blackboard/chalk, or newsprint or flip-chart paper and markers
> - retreat packets (copies of pages 187-190)—one per person, to be handed out after the opening devotion
>
> **Note: Every group member should plan to bring the following items to the retreat:**
>
> - a Bible
> - a pen or pencil
> - a notebook, some paper, or a journal

Opening Devotion—Dying or Thriving?

> **Supplies needed:**
> - a thriving potted plant
> - a dying plant, flower, or branch

Read John 7:37. Then share the following in your own words:

We want our lives to bear witness to the life-giving waters that flow within us. Yet we are often running on empty. Filling our spiritual tanks takes time and energy. We weren't designed with an auto-refill button, and our lives often reflect the results of an empty tank.

As you take a look at this plant (show the dying one), what do you see? What words describe it? (List those words on a whiteboard or chalkboard.)

Now take a look at this one. (Show the group the one that is thriving.) What do you see? What words describe this? (List these words on the board as well.)

Find one or two other people and talk through these questions

SECTION 6: Great Escapes

(you may want to write these on the board or make copies to distribute):

- Share a gardening story from your life.
- Do you have a green thumb? Why or why not?
- Compare the lists we created as a group and relate them to your life.

(Bring the group back together for a closing song.)

Extended Quiet Time

Following the opening devotion, you are just about ready to send your group out for this portion of the retreat. Before group members head off on their own, cover the following:

- If you haven't already, distribute retreat packets (copies of pages 187-190) to everyone in the group.
- Share directions and/or maps of places to go for complete solitude, as well as a map of hiking trails, if available.
- If your group is confined to a single, large room, consider playing soft instrumental CDs to provide some background music. Prepare a refreshment table of drinks and snacks if you desire.
- Explain to your group that the extended quiet time is divided into six sections: God's Invitation, My Expectation, Adoration, Meditation, Supplication, and Celebration. Each section has a Scripture focus, along with a question or two to reflect on or a suggested activity—except for the section titled Meditation. The Meditation section invites us to peek into the heart of God as we reflect on the living water he constantly offers to us. The goal isn't to complete this section, but to gladly receive what he longs to give us through the promises and truth of his Word.

In your own words, say: "It's time to head our separate ways. The first thing you'll find in your retreat material is a letter. Take the time to read it. It will set the stage and allow you to embrace all that God has waiting for you.

> ### *Retreat Packet Material*

Dear friend in Christ,

Welcome! Welcome to this quiet place. An unhurried, quiet afternoon isn't a regular occurrence for most of us. It may feel a bit strange, yet we're in good company. For centuries, when God's people were off alone, away from the familiar, everyday things of life, God had a way of making himself known in remarkable ways. God is the same today. With great care, he'll orchestrate these quiet hours to prepare your heart for all he has in store for you.

But first, it's important to relax and unwind. This isn't a race. You don't have to do anything. The goal of the next two hours is to simply enjoy being in God's presence.

If you're like most people, you're underrested and overstressed. One of God's gifts for you in the next few hours is rest. So do what you need to do to slow down. Focus on each minute, each hour. Take deep breaths. Take a walk. Listen for birds. Enjoy a cup of tea. Lie in the grass and watch the clouds. Wiggle your toes in the sand. Skip some stones. Follow an ant. Catch a frog. You are free to be, to rest, and to enjoy two hours of no expectations!

When you're feeling rested and ready, turn your attention to God. Invite him to come near, asking him to make you fully receptive to the Holy Spirit's leading.

Go where he leads. Dig into the retreat material. Read your favorite psalm. Reflect. Journal. Pray. Sing. Rest some more. You can use this guided retreat resource, but do so only if it helps you draw near to the throne of grace. Be still or move around—whatever helps you sense the closeness of God.

Welcome to this time alone with the Lord.

God's Invitation

Meditate on Isaiah 55:1-3. How are you hearing God speak these words to you today?

My Expectation

Spend some time studying Psalm 86:1-4. Sum up the meaning of each verse using your own words. Make it into a prayer. Whisper it to God or write it down.

Adoration

Read Psalm 95:1-7. Loudly or quietly, standing or sitting, allow your soul to magnify the Lord.

Meditation

Use Job 22:22 to prepare your heart to focus on the power of God's Word.

As you read on, you'll find four scriptural reflections on the "Living Water." For this time of meditation, you can use as many or as few of these reflections as you desire.

Reflection 1: *Drip. Drip. Drip.*

Where's the leak? Sometimes we find water where we don't want it. Other times, there's none to be found. Both floods and drought wreak havoc. But there is one source of water that endlessly supplies exactly what we need.

Pause, Praise, Ponder, and Pray

Read Jeremiah 2:13.

• In what ways do the words of this verse reflect your life?

• What's the good news implied in this verse?

Retreat Packet 2 • Page 2

SECTION 6: Great Escapes

Reflection 2: *Good News*

At different stages in our lives, we're more or less attuned to our flaws and failures. Where are you right now? Burdened by your sin? bored? blessed? When facing your faults, where do you turn?

Pause, Praise, Ponder, and Pray

Read John 4:4-14.

• How thirsty are you? What are you thirsting for?

• In everyday life, how do you approach God as the source of living water? Do you come with a bucket or a teacup?

Reflection 3: *Streams in the Desert*

We've all felt it—sunburned shoulders, worn-out sandals, scorching heat. We've all trekked through the desert at some point in our lives. It's not fun, but as we peek over the horizon, hope remains alive.

Pause, Praise, Ponder, and Pray

Read Isaiah 43:18-21.

• What "sand" is in your shoes that you need to shake out?

• How do you offer praise to God when he provides in unlikely places or at unlikely times?

Reflection 4: *Harvest Time*

An endless supply of living water is available to every Christian. It satisfies the thirstiest soul and provides all we need for a rich and plentiful harvest.

Pause, Praise, Ponder, and Pray

Read Isaiah 58:11.

• What fruit has God been growing in your life?

• Take a walk and find something from nature that depicts what God is doing in your life. Keep it close and bring it with you to the small group Bible study time. (Remember not to disturb anything that's alive!)

Supplication

As you come to the end of this extended quiet time, carefully read Psalm 141:1-2.

God longs for us to come to him with specifics. This breeds intimacy in your relationship with God. Lay your heart's desires before the Lord, trusting him to hear and respond as a loving Father. Pray, but don't neglect to quiet your heart and listen in response.

Pray for
• your family and friends, their burdens and cares

• your small group and the ministries of your church

• those you know who don't yet have a relationship with the Lord

• yourself

• your own burdens

• your dreams and desires

• your hunger for the presence of God

Celebration

Read Daniel 2:20-23.

Thank God for meeting with you in this place. Make a list of what he's revealing to you, what you're experiencing, and what insights you're gleaning from his Word.

When finished, gather back together with the group at the designated time and place.

Retreat Packet 2 • Page 4

Small Group Bible Study

Open with prayer.

Share the questions listed below with your group (you may want to post these on a board or make copies to distribute). Ask each person to select one or two of the questions and share their thoughts with the group.

- What did you learn about yourself today?
- What did you learn about God?
- How did he make himself known to you?
- How did you experience stillness today?
- What was most challenging?
- What aspect of this day was difficult?
- How did you experience the power of God?

In your own words, say the following:

"Life is full! Days are long. Most of us pack a lot of living into our weeks. It's easy to get depleted. Wearing out isn't a sign of emotional failure. We were created with a built-in need to rest and recharge. Yet we live in denial, surviving on too little sleep and too little rest. God wants to refuel us. The image of living water speaks volumes to our thirsty souls. Our lives depend on it!"

Read Psalm 65:9-13.

Circle around the group once or twice, having each person choose the question(s) he or she would like to answer from the list of questions that follow (you may want to post these on a board or make copies to distribute). Each question is linked to a specific verse that could be reread before the person shares his or her thoughts.

- **Verse 9:** What are three things that demonstrate God's goodness in your life? What are you thankful for today?

- **Verse 10:** Just as rain softens the ground beneath our feet, God uses many things to soften our hearts. Each of us has a unique

SECTION 6: Great Escapes 6

set of challenges, joys, circumstances, and relationships designed to soften our souls. What are some situations and people that God is using to drench, level, soften, or bless you in this season of life?

- **Verse 11:** What fruit of the Spirit would you like to see overflowing from your "cart" this week or month? What specific things do you need to do to make yourself more accountable, so that you may enjoy this bounty in full measure?

- **Verse 12:** What part of your life represents grassland growing in the desert?

- **Verse 13:** Which songs do your find yourself humming or singing when you're overwhelmed by God's goodness?

To provide a prayer focus for the close of this small group time, have group members share the nature objects they collected during the extended quiet time (as part of Reflection 4) that depict what God is doing in their lives right now. (Those who didn't do Reflection 4 may simply describe something in nature that would convey God's action in their lives.)

Lift up each person in prayer.

Closing Devotion

Plan a closing (using the suggested agenda that follows) that allows participants to come down from the mountain with a peaceful heart. Encourage each other to share your favorite verses about God's peace, provision, and protection. Worship the Lord with grateful hearts. For the closing devotion, use the images from the river of life found in Ezekiel 47:1-12. For this devotion, head to a lake, pond, or river. If it's warm enough, take off your shoes and wade into the water for your closing.

- Offer an opening prayer.
- Sing worship songs together.
- Read Ezekiel 47:1-12 and share your thoughts.
- Ask the group to share their favorite verses that speak of water.
- Sing more worship songs.
- To close, gather in a circle for prayer with toes in the water and holding hands.

TAKE CARE
Ways to Serve Beyond Your Group

SECTION 7: Table of Contents

7 SECTION 7: Take Care

Take Care—
Ways to Serve Beyond Your Group

Serving together can help your small group build a deep sense of community and friendship. Serving together expands the vision of your group and gets group members "outside of themselves." This section offers suggestions on ways your group can ready itself for serving others, as well as listing dozens of ideas for outreach projects within your church, community, and beyond.

4 BASICS FOR SMALL GROUP OUTREACH

As you get ready to dive into outreach as a small group, consider these basic "heart" principles for serving others.

1. Demonstrate your group's love and care

Learning how to be a caring small group takes time. People love to be with friends; they'll naturally seek out a warm, loving, and caring group. The best way to reach out is when satisfied people (your group members) tell others about the source of their satisfaction. A friend is the most influential means of bringing people to faith, reaching out through love and caring.

2. Use outreach to practice what you're learning as a group

Bible knowledge is important in your small group; but knowledge without life application is of little value. As you lead your small group, it's important to create ways for group members to put into practice what they're learning. Focus on helping create spiritual maturity in the life of the group's members (Colossians 1:28). This is vital as you think of serving others, because what we *believe* should determine how we *act* as Christians.

3. Make outreach a priority for your group

If you have no goals, you'll never know if you've reached them. Goals are simply what you reach for, something to help your group keep focus. Outreach needs to be a primary goal in your small group.

4. Be creative and innovative with outreach opportunities

In today's busy culture, you simply can't do business as usual. If you want your group to participate fully, outreach opportunities must be meaningful and practical.

10 QUESTIONS TO PREPARE YOUR GROUP FOR OUTREACH

As you plan how you'll reach out from your small group, these questions can help you make sure that you're prepared.

1. Does our group truly want to reach out to others?

2. Is our group committed to bringing new members into our small group (or birthing new groups) if our local service and outreach activities are successful?

3. Are we studying the biblical commands to reach out to others through acts of service?

4. Are we offering practical training to help our group members see the importance of outreach activities?

5. Have we evaluated the special talents and abilities of members of our small group and tried to discern how God can use those to serve others?

6. Are we providing training so that group members can best utilize their gifts in outreach activities?

7. Have we clearly targeted who we're trying to reach?

8. Have we made a list of the needs that exist around us so we can prioritize the most crucial needs and try to meet them?

9. Are we committed to respecting the time of our small group members, planning our outreach events so we don't waste our own time or the time of the people we're seeking to serve?

10. Have we sought the involvement of all group members in deciding what events to undertake?

6 PRINCIPLES FOR PLANNING A SMALL GROUP OUTREACH

The extent of planning necessary for an outreach project depends on the scope of what's going to be done. Shoveling sidewalks is far easier to plan than putting on a puppet show at a children's hospital. But in either case, poor planning can result in the work not being accomplished and leave you with a discouraged small group. Use these principles to help you plan.

1. Begin by evaluating your group

God has brought your group together. What has God equipped you to accomplish? Each person contributes experience, perspective, talents, gifts, abilities, and burdens. Take inventory of your group to determine what kind of service project you should do. A group made up of senior citizens probably shouldn't shovel snow. Don't try to build a shed for someone if no one in your group has any construction experience. Maybe anyone can make a joyful noise, but it takes musical talent to have joyful listeners on the receiving end!

Don't assume that you know everything about your group. Spend some time talking through the variety of skills and talents that exist in your group. This isn't a time for modesty. Consider using a written inventory to help those who feel awkward talking about themselves in front of the group.

To begin assessing what your group should do, answer the following questions.

- What is the age range of your group?
- What's their availability?
- Can they do physical work?
- Are they skilled in trades such as construction, plumbing, carpentry, painting, electrical?
- Would those who work in a trade want to also minister in the same way?
- Does your group have people who can cook or bake?
- Are there artists in your group? What kind of art do they enjoy?
- Is there an auto mechanic in the group?
- What are the burdens of the group? What issues touch their heart?

People are different. Some enjoy using the skills they use every day to minister. For others, the last thing they want to do is use the same skills that they use in their vocations.

Think of how different skills can blend together. Imagine a group made up of individuals who love drama, a seamstress, a carpenter, an artist, and a writer. Sounds like a drama or a play. Add a farmer, and you may have a living nativity.

2. Coordinate your project with church leaders

Check with your church's pastoral staff for special needs that your group can be sensitive to. Your church's leaders can help you determine who really needs help so that your service efforts will have the most meaning.

3. Consider a one-time service project

Some service and outreach projects are one-time events. You choose a date and everyone focuses on accomplishing the task at hand. After your group members have a few one-time projects under their belts, they may want to choose an ongoing service project.

This can be very rewarding—as long as everyone continues to work together. Long-term projects can easily disintegrate into one or two individuals keeping up with the responsibilities, and this can result in discouragement or even hurt feelings.

4. Choose a project that has an end time

Whether your group does a one-time project or takes on a task that lasts a year, it's wise to establish a time when the responsibility is complete and your group is able to enjoy a sense of accomplishment. After a time of reviewing things, you may want to continue the responsibility. But it's good to have that choice.

Also be careful of starting a project that will place a burden on your church leaders if your group decides not to continue its commitment. The people you serve can quickly get used to something, and then complain when it's no longer available. Make sure everyone knows that your small group will be undertaking this specific project for this specific length of time.

5. Start off with a small project

A smaller project will allow you to learn who the good leaders in your group are. Who is good at planning? Who is oriented toward details? Who is good at seeing "the big picture"? Who will work to see the project through to completion? Sometimes these qualities aren't clear until your group has worked together a few times.

6. Encourage participation from everyone

Be sure to talk about how important each person is to a task. Use the questions in number 5 ("Start off with a small project") as an example of the importance of each member of your group. When planning a project, make it a goal to involve everyone in the group.

30 OUTREACH OPPORTUNITIES WITHIN YOUR CHURCH

Building a tightly knit small group is not just helping group members develop spiritual intimacy; it's also encouraging fellowship and personal closeness. Often, as group members *do* things together, they tend to form bonds that last through the years.

Here are some ideas for service opportunities your small group can undertake right in your own church. By organizing and leading these events, group members will not only bless those who attend the events, but the act of working together, serving together, and having fun together will also deepen their relationships with each other.

1. Around the world in eighty minutes

Host a global awareness evening. You can either focus on world areas your church supports in missions, concentrate on the countries in one area of the world, or choose random nations that couples or teams of group members are interested in. Let group members do research to learn about the customs, culture, and spiritual focus of the areas. Offer an open house with booths featuring different world areas (complete with native dress, food, and customs) or create a program blending different presentations (drama, music, personal stories from people in those world areas, PowerPoint presentations, multimedia).

2. Let me entertain you

Have an old-fashioned variety show or talent contest. The focus can be for fellowship and fun—and getting to know each other better on a personal level. You can either let people sign up, or make them audition—whichever you feel would work best (and depending on how polished you want your show to be). If you want to be trendy, include categories like "useless talents" or "stupid pet tricks" as well.

3. Let the games begin

Host a night of games. Encourage parents and teens to play together (pull some ideas for group games out of youth group activity books) for at least some of the games, to encourage some intergenerational bonding. Have people bring a favorite game and their favorite snack.

4. Parents' night out

Depending on the ages of your small group members, they may remember how tough it is for parents with elementary-age and younger kids to get out. It's hard for married couples to have dates when they have younger kids—and with the combination of paying for a meal and a babysitter, just going out for an evening can be cost-prohibitive (especially at that stage when normal family expenses tend to be high). Instead of just a "moms' day out," host a "parents' night out" so that couples can get out together without the kids for a few hours, or so single parents can have a break in the evening. Inquire about using nursery rooms at your church—they're already childproof and have all the supplies you'll need. Ask the Christian education staff if the group members need to undergo any screening before caring for children.

5. Support group night

Put together an evening of support groups for the church. You can have specific support groups (like people battling cancer, parents with prodigal kids, and so forth) or general support groups (such as moms supporting moms, accountability for men). Your small group members are responsible for finding facilitators for the support groups. You could broaden this to once a week for a month, or turn it into a weekend event.

6. How to succeed in business by really trying

Host an evening or weekend workshop focused on business skills. Topics could include living out your faith at work and dealing with tough personalities in the office. Make sure this evening has plenty of practical take-home materials, and be sure to give it some spiritual focus because God cares about our work!

7. Sharing blood, sweat, and tears

The sweat is your small group's part. The blood (and a few tears when blood is drawn) comes during the blood drive organized and sponsored by your group and held at your church.

8. Holiday fest

The holidays can be a tough time for seniors and singles. Organize a party or outing for one of these groups. Rent a bus and see the best of the neighborhood lights or a special lighting display, or go caroling. Or you could have a special party at the church. The whole holiday season—from Thanksgiving to Valentine's Day—can be tough, so you could hold your party on any of the holidays within that time frame.

9. Rods for God

With the endless popularity of NASCAR and old cars, if you have car buffs within your church or community, host a car show. Let car aficionados bring their hot rods or cool cars to show off. Invite the fire department or ambulance services to bring their vehicles too. And for the fun of it, try to find a monster car. If you have enough cars, you could have a contest for best entries. Let local car and motorcycle dealers know about the show in case they'd like to display something, sponsor part of the show, or provide freebies or prizes for attendees.

10. Adult show and tell

Cars aren't the only things you can have a show with. Think about other interesting items or hobbies that several of your group members might be involved in, and consider offering a show. For example, during the holidays, have a display featuring unique nativity sets various people in the church own (you'd be surprised at how many people collect nativity sets). Or have an antique show where church members can display interesting pieces they're proud of. Look at the hobbies of your own group. Other possibilities include a garden show or a craft fair.

11. Beautify the church

As a group, take responsibility for improving the church landscape or doing minor remodeling projects. Does a Sunday school classroom or the library need a fresh coat of paint? How long has it been since the worship center chairs or pews were cleaned or waxed? What church kitchen doesn't need new shelf paper in the cabinets? Your group could offer a special ministry by tackling the small, neglected tasks that seldom get done. Be sure to get the proper permission first.

12. Establish a "telecare" ministry

A telecare ministry is a practical method of outreach. The members of your group call people who've been absent from church for a few weeks and members who are homebound. Work as a group and with your pastor, if possible, to come up with some basic scripts for appropriate words to say, as well as some helpful, practical guidelines for meeting needs.

13. Truly selfless

Can your group meet the needs of people from other churches? This might be as simple as providing a ride to church for a senior adult—even if that church isn't your own.

14. Simple needs

Look over the names of those involved in the ministries of your church. See if you can find people in need (you won't have to look very far), and then have your small group fill that need. Maybe this involves doing some shopping for a shut in, tackling some cleaning, or doing yardwork. Special activities like vacation Bible school or special events (family, Christmas, and Easter events, for example) are more formal ministries where your small group can creatively reach out and help.

15. "Muggers"

One church has a group they jokingly call the "Muggers." These are people who take a simple gift to first-time visitors—a gift of a coffee mug filled with candy, or small bottles of water. The Muggers make their visits early in the week and simply let first-time guests know they're appreciated. Your small group could use this creative idea to reach out to others.

16. Greeters and ushers

This isn't necessarily a new idea. The new aspect is for your small group to serve together as greeters or ushers for a period of time. Or perhaps you could help start or increase the church's parking lot attendant ministry.

17. Audio or video

If your church provides audio- or videotapes of its services, your small group could find out if any help is needed in preparing the tapes. Or maybe your group can take over delivering tapes to homebound church members and friends.

18. Friends away from home

When people leave on vacation or even extended travel, they can easily feel detached from your church. Your small group could take on a summer (or ongoing) project to keep in touch with church members who are traveling—sending e-mails, writing cards or letters, even calling if a crisis situation comes up at church.

19. House watch

Your small group members could offer the service of keeping an eye on church members' homes while they're away for vacation. This can be a simple drive-by check, or it can be more elaborate, such as watering plants and mowing the yard.

20. Small group day or weekend

To keep the needs and focus of your small group ministry before the congregation, have a "small group day" or "small group weekend." Think of this like a trade show—set up tables in the church foyer for your group and any others in the church that want to let people know the benefits of small group ministry.

21. Host the youth group

Throw a party for the youth group. Don't worry about trying to impress teenagers with how up-to-date you are (you'll be much "cooler" just being yourselves). Provide snacks, a home to meet in, and let the youth leaders do the rest.

22. Feed the youth group

Take responsibility for the kitchen on a youth retreat or mission trip. You really only need one or two people who can cook and plan the meals for a large group, but it takes a lot of helpers to pull it off. It's a big job, hard work, but very rewarding. Your group members will be co-laborers with the youth leadership in seeing God work in the hearts of young people.

23. Literature distribution

Distribute literature for one or more ministries at your church—the kick-off for the midweek children's ministry, the new service starting just for young adults, a holiday program or concert at the church, or the dates for vacation Bible school. Depending on the event, you could pass out information door-to-door or hand out material in a crowd.

24. College care packages

Get a list of the college students from your church and send them care packages. Include fun things as well as practical items. Homemade snacks and toiletries will be appreciated. Also include a "fifteen-second postcard." Stamp and preaddress a postcard to each student's parents, and add questions that allow the student to check the right answer or give brief answers. Make it informative as well as humorous.

For example:

School is going:

__ Great!

__ OK.

__ What school?

My number one prayer request is _____.

To Mom

25. Host a newcomers' activity

Create a special evening for people who are new to your church. An open house works great because individuals and families can drop by when it best fits their schedules. Work with the church leadership, and consider making it a quarterly event. Your group's job is to make people feel welcome, and help newcomers get to know people who've been around awhile.

26. Pastor appreciation

October is Pastor Appreciation Month. Honor your pastor by putting together a book of appreciation letters from group members. Make this an annual event. You could also invite the congregation to submit letters for the book. Say thank you to those who are responsible for leading you.

27. Oversee a church fellowship

Take responsibility for the planning and organization of a churchwide fellowship. This could be as simple as providing coffee and dessert after a service, or as elaborate as putting together a dinner theater. Your group doesn't necessarily have to do all of the work, but it should take overall responsibility for making sure the event is a success.

28. Adopt a missionary

Adopt one or more of your church's missionaries. Pray for them once a day. Write to them once a month. E-mail more often if that's possible. Be responsible for hosting them when they visit the church. You can even plan a short-term mission trip, with your group working together to raise the money to visit them (or to send one or two from your group to work with them). This will be a great encouragement. Remember that missionaries often have several churches and individuals supporting them. Make sure that your project encourages your missionaries rather than creating more work for them. Don't expect them to answer every e-mail or to write a thank-you note to your group every time you do something.

29. Anonymous church project

Talk with one of the church leaders and find a project that your group can take responsibility for. Think of something unusual: Replace the nursery furniture, buy a new deli-style slicer for the kitchen, or make curtains for the classrooms. Do the project and keep it anonymous.

30. Ask the pastor for the worst task

There's probably something at your church that no one wants to do. Straighten up a storage room or give the restrooms a makeover. Be a servant of the church by doing a job that needs to be done but that no one wants to do.

40 WAYS TO SERVE YOUR COMMUNITY (AND SOMETIMES BEYOND)

The next logical step with service and outreach is for your small group to move beyond the walls of your church to serve people in the community. These projects are simply about seeing a need in your community and then taking action to meet that need.

1. Yardwork for a day

Do seasonal yardwork for people with disabilities or senior adults in your community. Raking leaves in the fall or shoveling snow in the winter can be overwhelming for a homeowner challenged by age or illness.

2. Adopt a house

Take idea 1 ("Yard work for a day") a step further. Choose a disabled or elderly person's home and cut the grass for the entire summer or shovel the snow for the whole winter.

3. Domestic service

Through your local media, have you heard of a family facing some kind of crisis? Arranging for your group to do laundry, vacuum, or dust can be such a boost to someone who has spent most of the week at the hospital caring for an ill or injured family member. You can do this project just once or for as long as the service is needed.

4. Transportation service

Line up rides to help seniors with their errands or doctor visits. Your group could be collectively available to help out with rides for a single individual. Or, on a larger scale, you could be responsible for a ministry that connects drivers in your church with those in your community who need transportation.

5. Care baskets for new moms

New parents leave the hospital with arms full of gifts. But if your group checks birth announcements in your local newspaper, several weeks or even months have probably passed since the baby came home from the hospital. Assemble care baskets of formula, diapers, clothing, or other items for babies (with one or two things thrown in for Mom and Dad) and deliver the baskets to new parents.

6. New resident welcome packet

Your church can subscribe to receive a mailing list of new residents in the area. Check your Yellow Pages for local marketing firms and call around to see if they offer this. Put together a welcome packet from your church. Many local businesses will give you discount coupons to include. Add a personal touch by recommending restaurants or shopping secrets for the area. Make sure that your church leaders approve of everything that you include in the packet. Similarly, in most areas, sale transactions of residences are recorded in the local newspaper; your church can send a "welcome to the neighborhood" packet that would be useful for people moving from outside the area, or those just moving from another local address.

7. Help care for a child with special needs

Caring for a child with special needs is stressful and exhausting for the regular caregiver. As a group, consider receiving the necessary training to give parents of special-needs children an afternoon or evening out. Obviously, if you receive special training, you should plan on doing this more than once.

8. Handyman for a day

Assemble a work crew to take care of necessary chores for a single parent, an elderly person, or someone who is laid up. Be sure that you have the expertise to do an excellent job. Maybe only one person has the skill, but others can help. Break the job into smaller pieces. One or two people can acquire supplies, others can bring snacks, and everyone helps as they are able.

9. Auto repair

If you have any auto mechanics (professional or repair hobbyist) in your group, offer a service of auto repair for those who can't afford it. The rest of your group can clean the car or assist the car owner with necessary errands while the car is out of service.

10. After-school tutoring

Could you tutor students or even just help them with homework? Parents might be stretched with work, or perhaps the homework is beyond their abilities. This activity can build lasting intergenerational friendships.

11. Teach domestic skills to children

Arrange to host classes at your church for children—perhaps as an after-school program—and teach domestic skills such as cooking, sewing, and knitting. This is a great way to reach across generations to pass on skills you've learned.

12. Teach English as a second language

Sit in a local mall for an hour, and you'll probably hear more than one foreign language being spoken. Can your group members volunteer to teach English as a second language? Check into what community programs are already offered, or start your own classes or tutoring.

13. Teach adults to read

Offering this service can be a great way to help your church serve the community as well as have opportunities to make a difference in an individual's life.

14. Teach hobbies to children

Older adults can teach children how to play chess, paint, or even garden. This can be a great opportunity for intergenerational friendships and fun. Start a chess club or give six painting lessons. Is there a piece of ground at the church that can be used as a garden? Invite neighborhood kids or check with nearby schools and offer this as an after-school program.

15. Visit a senior adult care center

Visit a senior citizen center. Put together a program of music or a worship or devotional service. Even just a regular time when group members visit with residents will be appreciated.

16. Christmas caroling

If your group can sing (even a little bit), put together a caroling group. Don't just think of doing it on a single evening. You can carol multiple times in the month of December. The obvious way to do this is by going door-to-door. But many shopping malls or districts invite groups to carol. Consider wearing costumes from the Victorian era.

17. Homeless shelter

Volunteer to help out at a homeless shelter. There are a number of ways that you can be involved. Simply arrange to help out in any way that the organization needs you, or be responsible for collecting gifts and donations from others in your church.

18. Prayer project

Take on a prayer project. Pick out something to pray for—a block in the church's neighborhood, the high school seniors in your community, or visitors at the upcoming Easter services. Go beyond just mentioning something in prayer. Get together once a day or once a week for prayer. Coordinate praying around the clock for a day. Get group members to commit to praying on the hour every day at a specific time. It will be exciting to see God answer prayer.

19. Inner-city Christmas

Contact an inner-city ministry and ask if you can be responsible for giving Christmas gifts to needy children they serve. Collect names and ages of children. Make two kinds of Christmas ornaments, one for a practical gift and one for a fun gift. Write the name, age, and gender of a child on each ornament. Have people in your group or in the whole church take an ornament and bring back an unwrapped gift (so you can be sure the gifts are age- and gender-appropriate) for that child. Wrap the gifts and distribute them in the days before Christmas.

Or you can reach out around the world with the shoe box ministry of Samaritan's Purse. Set up a display and ask people to begin collecting boxes. Fill the boxes with children's gifts according to the simple instructions provided by Samaritan's Purse. Log on to www.samaritanspurse.org or call (828) 262-1980.

20. Beautify your neighborhood

Clean up a street, an abandoned property, or a neglected field. Check with local authorities for ideas and be sure that you're not doing someone else's job. The idea is to be a benefit to the community.

21. Pastor appreciation

During Pastor Appreciation Month in October, honor all the clergy in your community. Sponsor a prayer breakfast for senior pastors or all pastoral staffs; your group might be able to work with a local restaurant or catering company, as well as local media, to make this happen. This is a way to say thanks for the influence these leaders have in your community.

22. Service organizations

Members of your small group can volunteer to help local service organizations in your community. Your very presence speaks volumes. Some ideas: Boys and Girls Clubs, YMCA, Boy and Girl Scouts, chambers of commerce, Welcome Wagon, local schools—all provide rich opportunities to reach out in creative ways.

23. Helping hands

Picture your small group members scraping and painting a house for a needy family, rebuilding a porch, developing a park, or cleaning up a neighborhood. Select a major project that can be accomplished in four to five hours. Remember, many hands make light work. Your group doesn't have to do all the work—just take the lead and recruit other volunteers. This could become an annual event for your small group. Afterward, give a lot of positive recognition to those outside your group who participated.

24. Used-car ministry

Acquire used cars that aren't wanted, repair them, and either donate them to needy families or sell them and use the profit to help someone in need of transportation.

25. Professional advice

If you have lawyers, accountants, bankers, dentists, physicians, or other professionals in your small group, they can offer free advice to people in need in your community. Other group members can gather information, act as receptionists and assistants, provide snacks, and so forth.

26. Prison ministry

Are there ways your small group can get involved in prison ministry? Don't overlook your city or county jail, as well as providing services to families of those incarcerated (such as visiting, counseling, Bible studies). If it seems a bit scary to be involved directly with prisoners, you can still be involved in a ministry. Organize your church's efforts to minister through Prison Fellowship's Angel Tree project. This ministry provides gifts for prisoners' children at Christmas. For more information, check out Prison Fellowship's Web site: www.pfm.org.

27. School helpers

Call the principal of the nearest public school and ask how your small group can serve. It may take some convincing for him or her to realize that you don't want anything in return. And you'll really surprise administrators if you say your group is willing to do just about anything!

28. Special education

Special education teachers can often use volunteer assistants in their classrooms. Call the main office of your local school district to see who members of your group should contact.

29. Playground or lunchroom duty

Local public or private schools could probably use volunteers to help on the playground or in the cafeteria. Normally schools have well-established programs for volunteering. Check with a nearby school office for information.

30. Adopt a classroom

Perhaps someone in your small group knows a local teacher personally, or maybe a teacher attends your church. Can your small group adopt the classroom? Provide goodies for party days, decorate the classroom, and assist in the classroom or on field trips with administration approval.

31. Escort the elderly

Check with senior centers in your community and offer your small group for providing shopping escorts to local grocery stores and shopping centers.

32. Meals

Providing meals to homebound folks or people who are ill is another wonderful way to reach out. Check with Meals on Wheels or other local organizations (check the phone book) and offer to coordinate drivers from your small group.

33. Ministry to the hearing or visually impaired

Reading to elderly people who have limited sight or no sight at all is very fulfilling. Or visit with someone who has limited hearing. Of course, remember to speak slowly and loudly.

34. Hospital visitation

Your church may have a hospital visitation program for "friends and members" of the church. But chances are, a good number of hospitalized people would love the chance to visit with someone to help pass the time on long days in the hospital. Others may desire prayer. Check with the hospital office, as well as your own church office, to see if anyone has requested visits. Your group can serve as "lay chaplains" to supplement the work of busy local pastors and hospital chaplains.

35. Paperwork

Many people have problems with filling out forms, necessary papers, and tax forms. Perhaps your small group can offer a form service once a month at your local library. Or you could serve just once a year on selected days during tax preparation season.

36. Nursing Home VBS

Organize and conduct a vacation Bible school program in a nursing home! Those in the assisted living or nursing home cannot come to the church, so go to them. Keep it simple. Some singing, a short Bible story, refreshments, a simple game, and closing songs are all things you could do.

37. Lunch partners

Pair members of your group with homebound individuals and have lunch weekly with them. Your small group members can bring lunch into the home or, if the individual is able to leave the home, take him or her out to eat.

38. Substitute caregivers

Substitute caregivers stay with an ill or disabled person for a few hours each week, allowing the relative or caregiver a break from responsibility.

39. Help build a house

Habitat for Humanity provides wonderful opportunities for your group to get involved right in your own community. Contact Habitat to see what's going on in your city. Your small group can donate time to help build a house and/or provide or pay for materials for projects. For information, go online and log on to www.habitat.org/local to look up the nearest chapter, or call (229) 924-6935, ext. 2551 or 2552.

40. Ring a bell

The Salvation Army is a unique ministry, and it relies on many volunteers to keep up with all of its work. Your group could adopt a kettle and ring bells at Christmastime, or you could offer your service in more ongoing ways. For more information, go online and visit www.salvationarmyusa.org.

EXCEPTIONAL AND DISTINCTIVE
Ideas for Leading Specialty Groups

SECTION 8: Table of Contents

8

SECTION 8: Exceptional and Distinctive

Exceptional and Distinctive—
Ideas for Leading Specialty Groups

While it's easy to think of small group ministry as a program that spans the entire congregation, the reality is that small groups won't always represent a big cross section of your church. Sometimes the people who need a small group experience are unique—a group of men or women, or maybe singles or seniors.

The principles for starting and leading these and other types of affinity groups include many of the same principles for leading any small group. Still, special groups sometimes require special insight. This section offers helps for leading six different types of affinity small groups: seniors, families, free-market, men, women, and singles.

20 TIPS FOR SENIORS' GROUPS

Like people in other age groups, most senior adults love to be with friends and they love to chat! However, what makes senior adults different are their incredible lifelong experiences. Most senior adults love to share their experiences, and they have a lot to share. Small groups designed to meet the needs of seniors will allow seniors to share but, perhaps more importantly, will provide really meaningful times together.

Ideas for topics for seniors' small groups are limitless. If you hear senior adults talking about something, it's probably a good topic to discuss in your small group. Of course, on the surface, you'll think of topics such as retirement, personal health, friendships, transitions, losses, or concepts of aging. But don't be afraid to go beyond the basics and think creatively. Think of the twenty-first century senior adult. Consider some of these topics:

- Genetics and aging
- Between generations
- Abuse and neglect

- Home and community-based services for the elderly
- Care giving and community networking
- The challenges of aging in the twenty-first century
- Aging with grace
- Parkinson's disease, Alzheimer's disease, and cancer
- AIDS in the elderly
- Euthanasia
- Depression and loneliness
- Stresses seniors face
- Alcohol and drug dependencies
- Transitions to assisted living and skilled nursing care
- Hypertension and insomnia
- Stress and coping in later life
- Anxiety and panic attacks
- Codependency
- Sexual addictions

These are some of the issues that senior adult groups may have an interest in exploring. Your small group can engage seniors in discussions that will provide solid biblical answers.

Senior adults generally fall into two categories: active and inactive seniors. Some of these tips for small groups are overarching, while others apply specifically to either active or inactive senior adults.

1. Work within the ministry structure of your church

Check with the leaders of your church and share your vision for a senior adult small group (or multiple groups) with your senior pastor and pastoral staff. Ask how you should get started—where else you should present your vision and how to get any approvals necessary for making your small group(s) part of the overall ministry of your church.

2. Target your audience

If you're starting up a group for active senior adults, make sure that the group will cover topics that they'll relate to. The same is true if your small group will be geared toward inactive seniors—target their specific needs.

3. Make evangelism a key element of all seniors' groups

Reaching out to others has no age limit. An active senior may share her faith on the tennis court while the inactive senior may share his faith from his wheelchair in a care center. It's important that group members know from the very start that your group isn't meant to be "inward-focused" but rather designed for "outward focus." Groups should always be open to including new seniors. Certain groups may be dealing with very personal, confidential issues, and confidentiality is crucial; these groups may be closed for a season or may need to birth new groups after a specified term. But most seniors' small groups should simply be open and outward-focused in nature.

4. Set up your plan

Do you need to recruit and train any additional leaders? When will your group begin and end? How will you let people know about your group?

CROSS REFERENCE:
"6 Questions to Help You Promote Your Group," Section 1, page 14

5. Timing is important

Begin your small group at an appropriate time of the year. This is especially important with active seniors. For example, you might want to start meeting in the fall rather than summer when people are taking vacations. Similarly, schedule major activities for the entire year so group members know what will be happening and when. You may be surprised that people even plan vacations and trips around the small group's schedule—when people make a commitment and find needs being met, they tend to stay with it.

6. Keep each series at a reasonable number of weeks

For a group to just go on and on creates boredom. These groups can easily turn inward and exclusive. The longer the group stays together the harder it is to create new groups. The members begin to feel their group is a special, lifelong group. Make endings of your existing group and beginnings of new groups intentional.

CROSS REFERENCE:
"4 Best Endings for Small Groups," Section 2, page 78

7. Involve everyone in some way

This can be as simple as holding a potluck dinner where each person in the group brings part of the meal. This almost ensures that everyone in the group will be present. If you find yourself planning and organizing with the same few people—or worse, alone—change gears and get new individuals involved. Most people like to contribute, but sometimes you have to ask, rather than relying on the same few who volunteer for everything. Work to make everyone feel a part of what's going on.

8. Be practical

Your senior adult small group can meet some practical needs that no one else might even be aware of. Think about it. People who lose a spouse may become part of a bereavement support group, but a widowed man might also need to learn some practical skills such as cooking or doing laundry. A widowed woman may need the support of a bereavement group, but she may also need help with purchasing a new car or with maintaining her home. Yes, some of these topics sound stereotypical, but you'll quickly see if these and/or other concerns are the most practical needs within your group. Focusing on practical concerns doesn't have to be mundane—in fact, it can be a lot of fun.

9. The best gift you can give is yourself

When it comes to meeting the needs of inactive senior adults—those who live in retirement centers, assisted living care centers, adult group homes, hospices, or skilled nursing centers—one of the best ways you can help is with your presence. Just be there to lead the small group, share yourself, talk, hold a hand, laugh, pray, or read Scripture.

10. Always sign in when making your visit

If your group does meet in a care institution for seniors, be sure to check in with the front desk, information station, or nurse's station.

11. Heed the restrictions listed

Follow directions. If a "Do not enter" sign is posted, obviously you should *not* enter the room. That sounds so simple, but many people don't heed signs in care centers.

12. Wash your hands often

Each time you move from one room to another to chat with people, wash your hands every time, both before and after. If you are leading a small group in one room, wash before and after that group meeting. Many care centers have disinfectant dispensers right on the walls as you enter a room. Use them often.

13. Show real empathy

Empathy is feeling what another person feels. Both active and inactive seniors need to feel that you understand and care about them. Of course, that's not really different than any individual of any age.

14. Watch your time

Keep your small group time limited (preferably a short time). Be considerate of people's time. Active seniors may have full schedules that you're not aware of. Inactive seniors may get tired more easily and need extra rest.

15. Stay away if you're ill

This is true for both active and inactive senior adult groups. Your commitment to leading your group is admirable. But the one thing seniors do not need is germs! Don't pass on your cold, flu, germs, illness, or even your sour attitude.

16. Have a servant heart

As a leader, God calls you to serve and minister to others. Lead your small group prayerfully. Praying together bonds people. Develop friendships and let the Holy Spirit work in and through you.

17. Reach out

Reach out spiritually, emotionally, and physically. There is nothing quite like holding someone's hand when you're praying. Ask the group to hold hands during your prayer times.

18. Maintain confidentiality

It is important to not probe into personal matters, like medical or financial issues or what's going on in extended families. People will share what they want to share at their own time and comfort level. Always maintain strictest confidence.

19. Gracefully decline gifts

Sometimes, seniors become attached to leaders very easily. This is especially true if their families aren't close by. While your relationship is great, and it's wonderful that they begin to see your small group as a family, you'll want to keep all of those feelings at the appropriate levels. Because you're the leader of the group, you may be offered a gift; graciously express your appreciation, but decline.

20. Practice good communication skills

Empathize, pay attention, visit, and listen. Use good, clear verbal communication when you speak. Speak clearly and loud enough so everyone can hear you. Be upbeat and bring a positive message from Scripture.

Listen to what each person has to say. Listen as seniors in your group share about their losses. Listen for personal losses, material losses, and spiritual losses. They may talk about the loss of status or self-esteem. You may pick up issues of depression, anger, loneliness, fear, or rejection. There may be bitterness, unforgivingness, issues that just never were dealt with. Listen, listen, and then listen some more.

8 QUESTIONS ABOUT INTERGENERATIONAL AND FAMILY SMALL GROUPS

Have you ever wished that you could lead a small group composed of entire households and families? Why can't whole families pursue the same spiritual things together that individuals and couples do?

So many of our everyday activities (and church activities) separate us into specific age groups. But think how great it would be to come together on purpose to experience the benefits of multigenerational community life!

When multiple generations connect, a continuity of passing on faith occurs that can't happen when generations don't interact with one another. Modeling is an integral part of the process that God uses to transfer faith from generation to generation. Psalm 78:1-7 gives a beautiful picture of generations coming together and continuing to pass on the faith to future generations. When one generation does that for another, there's a much greater chance that future generations—even the children yet to be born—might someday know the Lord.

The following questions can help you determine if leading an intergenerational/family small group is right for you.

1. What are intergenerational/family small groups?

Quite simply, these small groups are designed for households or family units rather than for individual members of the household or family. These groups also go beyond just Mom, Dad, and the kids; they also include singles, single parents, grandparents, and others. The idea is to take a multigenerational approach to life and ministry, and specifically to your small group. The group focuses on equipping people to lead their families in a way that ministry happens through homes, to reach neighborhood and marketplace.

Intergenerational/family small groups are places where whole families and others worship, learn, pray, and fellowship together.

They offer the opportunity to participate with other families and others in the body of Christ in "family discipleship." If the process of discipleship can be summarized simply as "following Jesus," then family discipleship is "following Jesus in the context of a family."

The unique aspects of intergenerational/family groups are:

• They connect at least two generations for Christian growth.

• They're aimed at the entire family and age spectrum.

• They look different in every setting and situation!

2. What's the purpose of intergenerational/family small groups?

Again, these small groups function like other small groups, except they aren't divided because of generations or age. Essentially, the idea is to accomplish both the Great Commandment (loving God) and the Great Commission (making disciples) in present and future generations. And this takes place both in and through entire households.

3. What keeps us from trying these kinds of groups?

For one thing, they're different. Maybe they're not on your radar screen. Some common myths and misconceptions may also be keeping you from jumping into something new. These include:

• "Kids learn best from or with their peers."

• "Adults learn best from or with their peers."

• "Parents want or need a break from their kids."

• "We've never tried this before."

• "We don't know how to do this!"

• "There aren't any resources."

4. What are the benefits of intergenerational/family groups?

The benefits that come from creating small groups out of family units and other individuals are probably too many to list. But here are a few:

• Intergenerational/family groups bring families together rather than pulling them apart.

- These groups reconnect God's family and family members.
- Intergenerational/family groups provide opportunities for family discipleship.
- Again, Psalm 78:4-7 indicates that these groups please God.

5. What biblical principles and core values should intergenerational/family small groups embrace?

Biblical principles:
- Honoring God first. The family isn't an end in and of itself (Colossians 1:18).
- Reflecting the character of Jesus in our relationships (Ephesians 5:1; Colossians 2:6-7).
- Demonstrating fidelity in marriage (1 Thessalonians 4:3-7; Hebrews 13:4).
- Practicing chastity and purity in singleness (1 Thessalonians 4: 3-7).
- Nurturing the children God gives us (Psalm 127:3; Ephesians 6: 4).
- Showing lifelong care for family members (Ephesians 6:1-2).
- Maintaining a vital connection to a community of faith (Hebrews 10:24-25).

Core values:
- Jesus must have first place in everything, including family life (Colossians 1:18).
- Marriage between a man and a woman is a gift from God (Genesis 1:27-28).
- Children are gifts from God and welcome additions to the family (Psalm127:3).
- Our first ministry is to our family. We don't neglect them as we minister to others (1 Timothy 5:8).
- Parents are the primary teachers of their children (Deuteronomy 6:6-9; 2 Timothy 1:5, 3:14-15).
- In the context of family life, the church's role is to support the

home. If there is no Christ-centered influence, the church takes the role. Therefore, experienced Christians must teach and mentor (Titus 2).

- Christian community is inclusive of age groups (Joshua 24: 15; Hebrews 11), relational (1 Thessalonians 2:7-8), and interwoven (integrated).

---

6. Are there different types of intergenerational/family groups?

There probably could be as many different types of these small groups as there are families in churches. But here are a few common types of intergenerational/family groups:

Age-integrated home groups:
- Individual households/families observing daily worship times—spending time in God's Word and prayer (Deuteronomy 6).
- Two or three families meeting in a home. A family home group is one way to engage with your family and other families in activities that promote spiritual growth. It can also be an "equipping time" to provide you with resources to help you do these types of things regularly at home. These groups aren't easy—but what important thing in life is? Family home group meetings typically include the following elements: fellowship, worship, prayer, Bible teaching, "family time" (small group breakout), and food. In these groups adults and kids interact together—learning God's Word and getting to know him better together! This means activities need to be aimed to reach kids as well as adults. Families involved in the group lead sessions on a rotating basis.

Age-integrated church-based groups:
- Family discipleship Sunday school class or Bible study
- Fathers and Sons Together (FAST)
- Dads and Daughters (DAD)
- Mothers and daughters (MAGNET: Moms and Girls Nurturing and Encouraging Together)
- Mothers and sons

Groups during camps and missions trips:

- Camps, retreats, and family/intergenerational mission trips are great avenues for introducing these groups to your church. While in these settings, you can easily break a larger group into smaller intergenerational or family clusters for Bible study, prayer, worship, discussion, and meals. In this natural setting, people can easily see the simplicity and viability of these types of groups.

7. What are the best ways to start and keep intergenerational/family small groups?

Here are some basic principles to follow:

- Keep it simple! Remember that this isn't brain surgery. It's encouraging families and multigenerational groups to do the same things we encourage individuals and couples to do: Study God's Word, pray, sing praises to God, fellowship, and reach out.

- Believe it and live it! Encourage the leaders of your church to embrace, adopt, and model this concept. Recruit members of the pastoral staff and/or lay leaders and their families to commit to being a part of intergenerational/family groups.

- Don't propose that you replace age-segregated groups. Family and intergenerational groups are another option for people in your church; there's nothing at all wrong with people continuing in their more typical groups *and* participating in an age-integrated group as well.

- Plan for it! Help with wording that demonstrates how your church can weave family/intergenerational groups into the vision, values, and goals of your church. One easy way to do this is by encouraging whole households to do the same things individuals are encouraged to do.

- Integrate your "family group" into the church's overall small group ministry. Again, it's an option. A lot of people may not think to ask for this option, but some may choose these groups if given the opportunity.

- Focus on one-on-one recruiting of other small group leaders;

pray for and meet with people who share your desire to see family groups flourish.

- Pass it on! Communicate your commitment to the body. Encourage people in your sphere of influence to embrace, adopt, and model these groups.

- Keep the focus continually before people in your church. Use churchwide publications, the church Web site, platform announcements, and so forth. Tell success stories about your group through these methods.

- If your small group is successful, birth new groups. Encourage other thriving groups to spawn new groups.

8. What else do we need to keep in mind when it comes to intergenerational/family groups?

When you begin an ongoing group like this, communicate both subtly and clearly the reasons and expectations for having this type of group. Some suggestions:

- Encourage families to sit together at your meetings. Don't meet together only to segregate once you're in the same room or the same home.

- Parents are in charge of their own kids. No need for child care!

- As you lead and teach, resist the temptation to aim for the lowest common denominator. This isn't a children's group or an adults' group. Speak to all and apply what you're teaching to all ages.

- Remember that you're breaking new ground, and it will take your commitment and the commitment of the families and other individuals who give it a shot. It's not easy or simple, and it probably won't look "perfect." Offer each other plenty of grace.

The good news is that if your intergenerational/family small group is of God, he'll give you the strength, wisdom, and desire to lead. He'll work in and through you—and sometimes in spite of you—for his glory. Apart from Jesus you can do nothing (John 15: 5), but you can do all things through Christ who strengthens you (Philippians 4:13). Stand back and watch God do wonderful and awesome things through multiple generations!

6 BASICS FOR CREATING FREE-MARKET SMALL GROUPS

Do you enjoy playing basketball, making scrapbooks, leading a book study, or helping others with their finances? Have you ever considered the possibility that the thing you enjoy doing the most, the hobby or interest that you spend your "extra" time doing, or the thing that you do best just might be the passion in your life where you can find effective ministry?

Consider starting a small group around your passion—attracting others who share it with you.

That's the idea of "free-market" small groups. These groups are composed of a small group of people who share a common interest, a common need, or a common purpose, and they use that sphere of influence to disciple each other in friendship.

Here are some basic guiding principles for free-market small groups.

1. Let relationship occur naturally

The real key to effective ministry comes from forming relationships, more than from the content of the group. The shared interest, need, or purpose isn't the main focus of the group (even if it sometimes seems that way). Rather, it's simply the connection point for finding other people who share your interests. You're not just trying to form casual friendships; instead, you're aiming for purposeful relationships—like most small groups—where members have permission both to "warn" and "encourage" one another (1 Thessalonians 5:14). The connecting point of a common interest just gives group members a head start on relationship. This is important, because the more you know each other, the more you'll care for each other.

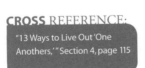

CROSS REFERENCE:

"13 Ways to Live Out 'One Anothers,'" Section 4, page 115

2. Assess where group members are spiritually

The first step toward building a small group around the interests you share with others is to make a sensitive, mental assessment of your small group members. Try to understand where each one is in terms of his or her spiritual journey. We're all at different places in our spiritual walks, and knowing where each member of your small group is along life's road will help you determine how best to move them forward. Ask yourself some simple questions about each small group member or potential member. For example:

- "What does he seem to think about God?"
- "What's her general outlook on life right now?"
- "What does he think about his future?"

You can only find the answers to these and other questions by getting to know your small group members—sharing fun times together and listening to what they're saying.

Once you start to understand the perspective of each member of your small group, you're ready to begin to implement some spiritual activity in the life of your group that will help move members forward on their spiritual journeys. Remember that, as a small group leader, you may be simply planting seeds in some, watering what has already been planted in others, and harvesting the souls of others.

3. Be intentional with adding spiritual components

Whether you like to play volleyball, read books, ski, sew, cook, study the Bible, or pray for a missionary—there are probably others who share that interest and would love to do it with you. You may be asking, "So what does playing volleyball or cooking have to do with ministry?" That depends! If you're intentional in your role as a small group leader, you can blend in a spiritual aspect each time you meet together. Some ideas:

- Pray together before you start playing volleyball or cooking. For some, praying is a new activity that will have more of an effect on them than you might think.

- Spend some time singing worship songs together—even if it's singing along with a good worship CD.

- Have a short Bible study. Or share favorite Scriptures and talk about how they apply to life.

- Ask a mature Christian in the group to share a short faith story of how Christ has influenced his or her life.

You might consider any or all of these ways to move your friends purposefully toward a more mature, successful Christian life. All of these steps are more meaningful in the context of friendship—people who care about one another and share life's ups and downs together. That happens most naturally with friends who share a common interest. But remember (yes, this is a reminder) that the content or activity of your small group isn't the most important aspect of your group; building God-honoring relationships is—intentionally helping each other move forward toward God.

4. Keep the purpose of the group clear

Building a small group around your own interests and passions can be fun and fulfilling. However, never look at your small group as a prospective business. When you decide to build a small group around an interest, you must be motivated by the desire to serve and minister, not to sell something. In practical terms, don't let your small group meetings become a place to trade business cards, to sell things, or to add people to a marketing network. People will feel taken advantage of and be offended if these things happen in your now *quickly shrinking* small group.

5. Keep in line with your church's vision

Seek the counsel of the person in charge of small groups at your church—the pastor, the small group or discipleship pastor, the lay person who serves as the small group leaders' coach. Serving under the authority of your local church is key to successful small group leadership, and you should always stay in line with the vision and philosophy of your church.

6. Be careful with finances

Never collect offerings or money in your small group without a clearly stated purpose. Your church already collects offerings during the weekend services, so you shouldn't need to collect offerings in your small group. Occasionally, you may become aware that someone in your group is financially in need. If you decide to help this person financially, take great care to collect funds openly and honestly. Ask another group member to count the money with you, or better, recruit two or more group members to head up this short-term relief effort. Make sure your group hears a report about the needs they were able to meet—at the same time, protecting the integrity of the group member in need at all times.

When it comes to finances, it's also wise to stay clear of committing your small group to any financial obligations and fundraisers. Generally, money and small groups don't mix well. Money is the obstacle that can most easily hinder your small group from developing solid, trusting relationships.

So think about your interests, your hobbies, and the things in life that make your heart beat faster—the things that you do the best. Or think about the needs that might exist in your church congregation, neighborhood, or place of employment. Whether your passion is fly-fishing, playing hockey, helping couples strengthen their marriages, or helping young couples with young children learn how to be good parents—all of these ideas can be tools that God can use to strengthen others, move the church outside its four walls, and bring people to Christ. Step out and be willing to lead and influence others who might share that same interest, and watch God begin to use you in their lives!

12 PRINCIPLES FOR MEN'S SMALL GROUPS

Small groups provide an optimal place for men to grow and become what God desires them to be. In small groups, men can find support, encouragement, accountability, and prayer. This environment helps men shape their character, hone their skills, and enlarge their worldview.

Within the context of a small group, a man who is struggling with anger, the loss of a job or spouse, an addiction to the Internet, or a darkness in his walk with the Lord has the opportunity to share his struggles, hurts, concerns, dreams, and victories. The other men in his group can stand with him, encouraging, cheering, comforting, and supporting him as they walk through life together. Of course, it doesn't always work this way in churches today. We end up judging each other and acting phony in front of one another, trying to give the impression that we're "good" Christian men. But when men in small groups start to relate to each other the way God intended— experiencing trust, authenticity, and honesty—they'll feel free to share who they are and what's going on in their lives.

Here, based on men's uniqueness and design, are twelve principles for leading a small group for men.

1. Provide "safety"

Most men love to go into their "cave" when they're frustrated, angry, or trying to figure out something. They view space as safety, but see closeness or intimacy as a threat. By nature, men are independent.

You'll need to allow the men in your small group a lot of time for the walls to start coming down. They'll need to be willing to open up and share with each other from their hearts. This will be a gradual process. Your group needs to be a place where the trust level goes up, so that group members are willing to share the deeper issues of their lives. Spend time sharing with each other about easy issues. For example, share with the group your own most embarrassing moment in life before you were eighteen, and ask them to share theirs too. Week by week, your discussions can go deeper.

CROSS REFERENCE:
"50 Questions to Deepen Group Relationships," Section 4, page 120

2. Start and finish on time

For men, time is money. They're used to the standards of the marketplace, where meetings usually start and end on time, are well planned out, and make a clear point. If you say your small group meeting will be from 6:00 a.m. to 7:30 a.m., then start at 6:00 and end at 7:30. This shows your respect for their time. If something comes up and some members of your group want to stay and talk, that's fine. But officially end your meeting and allow those who need to leave to do so without feeling guilty.

3. Be challenging

A lot of men see just about everything around them as something to be overcome and conquered. Most men are sick and tired of just talking about sports and the weather; they want to go deeper and be challenged. As you ask men to be in your small group, make sure they know what the commitment is and how much time it will take to do the homework. Men will extend themselves if they know what the goal is and what they will get out of it. They want to be involved in something significant and life-changing.

4. Get to the "bottom line"

Men like material at the bottom shelf, meaning that they want to move from theory to practical application. They want to know how the topics your group is discussing apply to their home, workplace, and community. As a leader, it's easy to keep your small group at the theory level and never "land the plane." To overcome this, when you're promoting your small group, make sure the proposed topics are stated in a way that will describe how those topics apply to them as men. Also, as you plan your small group time, make sure you reserve at least ten or fifteen minutes for group members to discuss how the study is relevant to their own lives. Have the men pair up and take five minutes to share with each other how they see the discussion applying to them, as well as one way they can apply the material during the coming week.

5. Provide opportunities to "win"

One of the greatest fears men have is the fear of failure. By nature, most men are very competitive, and this leads to comparing themselves with other men. While this is natural, it can greatly hinder relationships and the feeling of community in your group. As a small group leader, you can help by taking care not to put a man in a position where he doesn't know an answer and has to admit that to the other members of the group. Start with easier questions—perhaps ones that are just opinion and don't really have right or wrong answers. As the men in your group gain some confidence, you can move on to harder topics. The same is true if you plan a service project for the group—tackle something that your group will succeed at with the men and time you have.

6. Foster healthy ways to share emotions

Most men today don't have a clue what's going on inside emotionally. Even fewer know how to express their emotions in a healthy manner. A lot of men funnel their emotions through anger.

In order for men in your small group to start sharing what's really going on emotionally, they need three things:

- A safe environment. Your group needs to become an environment where there is trust, acceptance, and confidentiality.

- A model of what healthy expression of emotions looks like. As the leader, you can show members of your group what it looks like to share in a healthy way at an emotional level. Many guys have never had this modeled for them.

- Adequate time to talk. You can't demand that someone has to be vulnerable with his emotions. You can be subtle (but still sincere). As group members talk about what's going on at home or work, simply ask, "How does that make you feel?" If they are unsure or can't identify the emotion, you can provide some options. For example, if someone shares that he lost his job, you can ask, "So, how do you feel about this?" He may respond, "I don't know" or "I feel bad." Follow up by asking, "Would you say it makes you sad or angry or scared?" Gradually, this will help the men in your group begin to identify and express what they're experiencing emotionally.

7. Provide starts for the healing process

Many of the men coming into your small groups have wounds: father wounds, mother wounds, a divorce wound, or a work wound. Most of them are probably using some form of anesthetic in an effort to feel better. The salve may be a socially accepted one, like work, gambling, or acquiring more and more toys. Or it might not be acceptable, like a sex addiction or alcohol and drug abuse. No matter what numbing effect they're trying to apply, the wounds are still wounds, and they're not dealing with healing—they're just trying to mask or minimize the pain. As a small group leader, you can watch for these wounds and observe how the men in your group are covering them up. As you learn of these problems, you can take several courses of action:

- Get together with the individual and talk to him about what you're hearing or seeing; provide some resources for him to address the problem. Because the guy has already established a relationship with you, he may be more open to hearing from you than from anyone else in his life.

- Refer the wounded individual to a professional counselor in your area who can help with the issue he's facing. Talk to your pastor and ask for help in compiling a list of counselors.

- Provide support groups for men struggling with various issues. For example, sexual addiction is common among men in today's culture; you could offer a support group for men who are struggling with Internet pornography or other sexual issues.

8. Address workplace issues

The average man spends fifty to sixty hours at work each week; for most guys, work is major component of their lives and identity as men. Too often, the larger church doesn't address work issues, so it's easy for men to assume that their faith and their work worlds are two separate aspects of life. Your small group can be a place where you find out what the Scriptures say about living out life and faith in the marketplace.

The men in your group will probably be surprised to learn what the Bible has to say about work. For example, most of the characters in the Bible are marketplace Christians. Joseph was the first commodities broker; Daniel was in politics his entire life. Check your local Christian bookstore for resources on the subject of work and Christianity that your group can go through together. By teaching men how to apply their faith to the marketplace, you're dealing with an issue that is central to them as men.

9. Provide action

Most men love to be doing something, and they measure themselves by what they get done. Doing something together can also help them develop good relationships. Working side-by-side can quickly become face-to-face sharing about something important.

To cultivate this phenomenon in your small group, plan a service project once or twice a year to get the men in your group out of their normal settings to work on something together. This could be helping at a soup kitchen, doing a project in the summer with Habitat for Humanity, or helping elderly people from your church get ready for winter. These projects will go a long way in developing the relationships between the men in your group. It gives them something to look forward to and something to talk about when done.

CROSS REFERENCE: "30 Outreach Opportunities Within Your Church," and "40 Ways to Serve Your Community," Section 7, pages 201 and 209

You can also use men's natural tendencies to be in action by introducing experiential learning into your small group. Rather than spending all your time discussing topics or chapters at your meetings, come up with activities you can do, in your group setting or outside of it, to make the spiritual principles more interesting and applicable. For example, if you are discussing prayer, take your group on a prayer walk through the church or your neighborhood. If you're talking about how men grow to be more like Christ, have them storyboard their lives and share with the group. These types of activities will keep the men interested.

CROSS REFERENCE:

"12 Practical Ways to Live Out What You've Learned," Section 5, page 141

10. Guide men to other small groups that "fit"

Contrary to popular literature claiming that men are from Mars, men aren't all alike. The same type of small group won't fit everyone. Some men need an entry-level group because they're just getting started, and six weeks is all they feel comfortable with. Other men may be looking for an accountability group where there's no Bible study, but just a time to share what's going on in their lives and then pray for each other. Others need the equipping that a training-type small group can provide. Still others who are dealing with difficult issues in life may need a support group more than anything else. There are many types of small groups; guide guys to the groups that fit them best—even if those groups are sponsored by a different church!

11. Share leadership

Share the leadership of your small group. These groups are a great place to develop leaders, and by giving other men a chance to lead, you're providing valuable on-the-job training. You're training them in a setting where they feel safe and will be accepted even if things don't go great.

You might start by asking if someone in the group would like to lead one of the group's meetings. When a guy volunteers, you can get together with him and help him develop the Bible study or discussion questions and provide a few pointers on leading the group. After he leads, make sure you touch base either on the phone or in person to go over how he did.

12. Meet outside of church

A lot of men feel uncomfortable inside a church building. This holds true even for guys who've been Christians for a long time. In some ways, a man has to become everything he's not when he walks into a church. Most men feel much more comfortable in a rec room or a boardroom. Try to find a restaurant that offers a separate room for meetings, or see if one of the men in your group works at a place where there's a conference room your group can use. Keep in mind that you'll want to minimize distractions so the men in your group can openly share, discuss, and pray together. Trying to do this in the middle of restaurant with people coming and going probably isn't a good idea.

Starting a small group (or groups) for men can be a demanding but exciting challenge. You're offering men the opportunity to relate to each other in healthy ways, to openly share who they are, and to talk about what's going on in the deepest parts of their lives.

6 WAYS SMALL GROUPS CAN MEET THE NEEDS OF WOMEN

Small groups are ideal settings for women because they foster relationship building and sharing. Small groups can be wonderful places to meet the unique needs of women—if you realize that a women's small group isn't just any old group with a "women's" label slapped on.

If you use your small group ministry to truly give women what they need, you can have a dynamic, growing, thriving ministry. You'll not only provide a ministry that women in your church are looking for, but you'll attract the attention of women living around your church. And those who are involved will want to bring their friends, too.

Here are some of the major needs women have and how you can lead a small group for women to help meet these needs.

1. Women need relationships

Intimate relationship with others is a driving force in a woman's life. Women have a deep craving for close ties with family, a circle of good friends, co-workers they can talk to, and compatible people at church to share their faith with. Remember in high school when the girls would always go to the restroom in groups, while the guys would always go alone? That illustrates how most women think at every stage of life. Of course, they sometimes need time alone to recharge, but their identity, status, and confidence are all based on the relationships in their lives. To build relationships in your small group for women, keep these things in mind:

- Allow for plenty of discussion time. It's fine to lead with your own teaching or to invite someone speak to your small group. But you must also allow time for the women in your group to discuss what's been said with each other. This is how they process information and figure out how it applies to their own lives.

- Allow for plenty of fellowship time. This casual time will help women find other women in your group with similar interests, and that will lead to deeper friendships.

- Consider pairing up the women in your small group as special "buddies" during the church year. This will help build interesting and fruitful relationships between women who may not naturally become friends on their own.

2. Women need to be loved and valued

Media and cultural pressure often cause women to feel that they don't measure up to some artificial standard that they think they should meet. Your small group is a great place to provide confirmation that they're valuable just the way they are—both to other people and to God. Here are some ways you can extend that affirmation:

- Make a database of all the women in your ministry. Include the details of their lives that are so important to them—their birthday, spouse's name, anniversary date, kids' names and ages, and so on. Use this information to send cards or small gifts on special occasions, or simply for conversation the next time your group gets together. When you remember and acknowledge the important people and dates in a woman's life, it demonstrates that you value her.

- At every small group meeting, let each woman know how happy you are that she came. Having an hour-long or two-hour get-together may not seem like a big deal, but when you consider that the women have to plan child care, meals, kid shuttling, and other tasks just to get there, they can easily come to the conclusion that it's not worth it. That's much less likely to happen if you regularly and sincerely tell them that their presence is valued.

- Hold Bible studies that focus on God's love. Show the women in your group how much God loves and values them—for who they are, not for how they look or what they do.

3. Women want practical help in all areas of their lives

As constant multi-taskers, women want to know how to make the most of the time, money, and energy they have to get everything done. They're also striving to be the best wives, mothers, daughters, friends, and workers they can be! By helping them in practical ways in your small group setting, you'll show that you care about them as whole people, not just as a check mark in the spiritual victory column. Here are some ways to show you care:

- Offer discussions on marriage, child rearing, discipline, time management, cooking, crafts, education, finances, and more, in addition to Bible studies in your group. Unless your small group is just for stay-at-home moms, offer topics for women at various stages of life—working women, single women, senior women, divorced women, and others.

CROSS REFERENCE:
"6 Small Group Child-Care Solutions," Section 1, page 25

- Provide child care, if possible, during your small group meetings so that moms don't have to find their own child care or keep track of their kids.

- If you can't provide actual resources relating to your small group discussion, at least try to provide direction for those who want more information. Making available a list of books or Web sites, copies of magazine articles, or the contact information for relevant organizations shows that you truly care about helping women with the topic you're covering.

- Study Christian how-to books as a group. Consider books on motherhood, women in the workplace, marriage, and more. You'll gain real-life wisdom from the books, from each other, and from God's Word.

4. Women need to express themselves

Women process experiences and emotions by talking about them, so give them opportunities to do that in your small group setting.

- Allow plenty of time for sharing prayer requests. Women can develop an incredible intimacy with each other as they share what's happening in their lives and then pray for each other about those happenings.

CROSS REFERENCE:

"13 Approaches to Group Prayer," Section 1, page 48; and "6 Ways to Make Group Prayer More Meaningful," Section 5, page 137

- Ask for feedback on the topic you're discussing. Allow women to share their opinions and comments, and let them know you value their contributions.

- Again, fellowship and discussion times let women share their emotions and lives with other women around them.

5. Women need to feel that they belong

This need is somewhat of a combination of other needs. Women want to feel a sense of community and relationship, and they want to feel like they're an important part of your small group. Some ways to reinforce a feeling of belonging include these:

- Send out an e-mail update to members of your group. Of course, the content is important. But at least as vital is the subtle message that, because they're included in what you're sending out to others, they're valued as a part of the group.

- Ask those who seem to be on the fringes of your small group to help. Ask one woman if she'll coordinate the snack rotation. Ask another if she'll be in charge of sending birthday cards to group members. It doesn't have to be a large responsibility (unless you're looking for someone to fill such a role), but having a job to contribute will help these women feel like a part of the group.

CROSS REFERENCE:

"7 Roles to Get Group Members More Involved," Section 2, page 69

6. Women need encouragement

Women are often overextended physically and emotionally. Think about it—many of the things that are relegated to women are thankless and constant: laundry, dishes, and houses get dirty as soon as they're cleaned. That fact alone can be discouraging. So women need to be built up by others and hear that they're doing a good job at all the things they're trying to accomplish.

- Choose Bible studies that are uplifting and encouraging. Study God's promises, how God used women in the Bible for great things, or God's love and care for us.

- Be careful about how much time you ask members to devote to your small group. While you want to get together on a regular basis, you don't want to schedule so much time together that it becomes difficult to keep the commitment to the group. Overly full schedules pave a quick road to discouragement.

CROSS REFERENCE: "12 Ways to Encourage Each Other Outside of Meetings," Section 4, page 124

- Keep a stash of funny, encouraging, "thinking of you" cards and envelopes. When you see someone in your group who could use a pick-me-up, send a card with a short note to say you're thinking about her.

12 TIPS FOR LEADING SINGLES' SMALL GROUPS

If you want to lead a singles' small group, it is important for you to understand who singles in the twenty-first century are. While single adults reflect people from every life stage—from young adults to seniors, from never-married to divorced or widowed—Christian singles can generally be divided into three groups: "Hopers," "Satisfieds," and "Kamikazes." While the ages of individuals within these groups can overlap significantly, Hopers typically span ages 18 to 26; Satisfieds, ages 27 to 35; and Kamikazes, ages 36 and beyond. Once you know a little more about these three types, you can quickly determine the makeup of your small group. This will help you understand the way members of your group think, and it can help determine what types of material your group needs to study.

Hopers don't want to be single, but everything around them reminds them that they are. They have a sense of urgency regarding marriage that's easy to pick up on. They've always dreamed about marriage and can't imagine a future without a spouse. They probably don't like Valentine's Day. They struggle to listen to sermons that deal with marriage or strong family life. They have head knowledge about being complete in Christ, but they'll readily tell you that they won't feel satisfied until they find a spouse, so they continue to hope for one.

Satisfieds would prefer to be married, but the fact that they're single doesn't totally occupy their minds and it doesn't define who they are. Instead, they're focused on discipleship, service in their church, missions, and their careers. They value extended family and their place in it. They're not all that bothered by sermons on marriage. Quite simply, they're satisfied with being single for this season in their lives.

Kamikazes tend to have a passion for discipleship, service in their church, missions, and any activity that they believe God is calling them to be involved in. Kamikazes have come to see their singleness as a lifetime calling from God, and they dive headlong into activities and ministries with no regard for what the future may hold. They may even sacrifice career advancement, chances to "earn a decent living," or the comfort of staying close to home. Kamikazes don't feel incomplete and can even take offense if anybody suggests that they might be.

Don't think of these differences based on different levels of spiritual maturity. Instead, realize that God may simply be calling singles in these three different groups to do different things. For example, Hopers believe that their strong desire for marriage comes from God, so it's natural for them to think about marriage more often than Satisfieds or Kamikazes do. Likewise, Satisfieds aren't less mature than Kamikazes simply because they still desire marriage and Kamikazes don't. Regardless of where someone "fits" (or doesn't) within these general types, keep in mind we are all made by God and that he has different plans for each person.

With these thoughts about different types of singles in mind, how can you put that knowledge into practice in singles' small groups?

1. Pray for wisdom

Before your group meets each week, set aside time to pray for wisdom (James 1:5). No matter how prepared you think you are for each meeting of your small group, you're going to hear about needs, struggles, and attempts to understand God's will from singles—most likely in ways that you can't possibly be prepared for. So spend some serious time conferring with the Source of all wisdom before you attempt to address such serious topics.

2. Use icebreakers

When starting a new small group or when new people join your group, ask an icebreaker question so members of your group have a chance to get to know a little about each other right away. Ask questions like, "If you could meet a Bible character other than Jesus, who would that be and why?" Or you can use less threatening questions such as, "What is one of your all-time favorite books or movies?" or "What summertime activity do you enjoy?" (Many icebreakers created for general small groups work equally well or can be adapted for use in a singles group.)

CROSS REFERENCE:
"10 Easy Warm-Ups," Section 1, page 32

3. Pray a prayer of adoration

As the leader, you can set the tone for your group's entire meeting by starting with a prayer of adoration. Pray one of the praise psalms or simply offer a prayer of adoration from the heart—thanking God for who he is, for what he does, and for his patience with each of us. Be specific in your prayers. Cite examples of God's faithfulness, provisions, and mercy. Specific prayers of adoration take the focus off your group and place it on God.

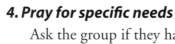

4. Pray for specific needs

Ask the group if they have any prayer requests—these can be related to anything from asking for strength to endure temptation to finding a new job. Write down the requests and ask the group to pray for each other collectively. Watch your list to make sure every request is prayed for, and jump in if a

CROSS REFERENCE:
"6 Ways to Make Group Prayer More Meaningful," Section 5, page 137

request is missed. Nothing will make individuals feel more loved by your group than to have one or more people pray for them.

5. Promote a sense of safeness

Many singles are hurting from breakups, divorces, the death of a spouse, or various other painful situations that they need to talk about. They need a place of safety to discuss their pain. Make it clear that your small group won't tolerate gossip, and that discussions and conversations containing personal information won't leave the room you meet in. If you ever have clear evidence that someone violates this policy, you may need to remove him or her from the group.

6. Pick relevant Bible study material

People join groups for one reason: They have a need to be met. Some join for knowledge, some join for social reasons—either way, they have a need and they're hoping your small group will help meet it. The Bible study material you choose for the group must give them the knowledge they need to overcome the struggles they face every day. Use materials that deal directly with struggles that are common to all singles—like loneliness, sexual temptation, unfulfilled expectations, and God's timing.

7. Read biographies about Christians singles

Inspire your group by having them read biographies about Christian singles who've made an impact on the world for Christ. Prepare discussion questions for each reading assignment. A few suggested books are *A Chance to Die: The Life and Legacy of Amy Carmichael,* by Elisabeth Elliot (Grand Rapids MI: Revell, 1987); *Movers and Shapers: Singles Who Changed Their World,* by Harold Ivan Smith (Grand Rapids, MI: Revell, 1988); *Prisoners of Hope: The Story of Our Captivity and Freedom in Afghanistan,* by Dayna Curry and Heather Mercer (New York: Doubleday, 2002).

8. Stress the positive aspects of singleness

Singles can easily drag each other down, particularly when it comes to focusing on their singleness. Occasionally, you might want to remind your group that "single" isn't the only word that describes them. One exercise you can use is to ask each member of your small group to write a one-page answer to this question: "What do I have a passion for right now that I could only do with my whole heart as a single person?" Either let group members work on this at home for a week, or give them ample time to write out their answers during your meeting time. Ask volunteers to read their answers. After people are finished, give the group an encouraging push to pursue those passions as if they were God-ordained—because they just might be!

9. Encourage service

Don't let your group focus solely on their own needs—even if that's the main reason they've come to your group. Christianity is about dying to self (Matthew 16:24-25). Suggest that your group volunteer at

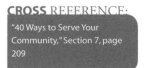

a church, community center, or neighborhood cleanup. You might even want to schedule repeatable and periodic service opportunities, like monthly or quarterly visits to homeless shelters, nursing homes, or hospices. Your group will quickly find out that their needs will be met as they serve others.

10. Encourage accountability

Explain the importance of confessing sins to each other (James 5:16) in a safe, nonjudgmental relationship. Offer to pair up willing people of the same gender as accountability partners, or encourage group members to choose partners. One key for this to work is that you don't force anyone to take an accountability partner—and you don't allow your group to know who does and who doesn't have an accountability partner. Some group members may already have this built into their lives outside your small group.

11. Look for and discuss singles' trends in pop culture

As you read the newspaper, watch television or movies, or observe people in your daily life, take note of trends that affect singles and think about what the Bible has to say about them. Use your observations as an icebreaker question to get the group started, or tie in your observations with a Bible passage that your group is studying. Look for trends and statistics on topics like cohabitation, promiscuity, dress, dating and courtship, and new genres of literature written just for singles.

12. Encourage social outings

Christians don't struggle to live faithfully for Christ nearly as often in church or group environments as they do in the "in-between" moments of their lives. They tend to struggle more when they're alone. Because singles live so much of their lives by themselves, they're even more susceptible to struggles. By encouraging your group to organize outings to the local zoo, the movie theatre, or restaurants, or to just get together to play board games, you help your group members to stay strong in the faith.

CROSS REFERENCE:
"22 Fun Small Group Activities," Section 3, page 89

SECTION 8: Exceptional and Distinctive

Appendix

Group Publishing's Small-Group Resources

HomeBuilders Couples Series®

This best-selling series, designed especially for couples, encourages spouses to grow closer to each other, to other couples, and to God. Each course has six or seven sessions, including a date-night feature that couples are encouraged to do between sessions. Brought to you by Group and FamilyLife.

- Building Teamwork in Your Marriage
- Building Your Marriage (also available in Spanish)
- Building Your Mate's Self-Esteem
- Growing Together in Christ
- Improving Communication in Your Marriage (also available in Spanish)
- Making Your Remarriage Last
- Mastering Money in Your Marriage
- Overcoming Stress in Your Marriage
- Resolving Conflict in Your Marriage

HomeBuilders Parenting Series®

This series offers encouragement and support to parents. There are six six-session courses to choose from. In addition to the group Bible study sessions, also included are date-night projects for couples and parent-child interactions for the family. Brought to you by Group and FamilyLife.

- Building Character in Your Children
- Establishing Effective Discipline for Your Children
- Guiding Your Teenagers
- Helping Your Children Know God
- Improving Your Parenting
- Raising Children of Faith

Group's Scripture Scrapbooks™

This is an exciting Bible study project for women's groups. We've combined scrapbooking and thought-provoking devotions. Come together with your group to grow in your faith and to scrapbook!

- Christian Living From A-Z (26 weeks)
- Fruit of the Spirit (10 weeks)
- God's Good Gifts (12 weeks)

Group's Out-of-the-Box Bible Studies™

Unlike any other small-group resource you've experienced before! This unique Bible study resource comes in a can and takes an experiential, hands-on approach to help people grow in their relationship with Jesus and have fun in the process—great for young adult groups. Each course is six sessions and contains materials for up to ten participants. Components include leader guide, gizmos, DVD, and more.

- Surprising Encounters With Jesus
- Surprising Things Jesus Said

And coming soon—scheduled for release in June 2005:

- Surprising Power of Jesus
- Surprising Questions Jesus Asked

Learn It, Live It Bible Studies®

Experience what God can do through a group that is willing to put their faith into action! In addition to the Bible study portion of each session (Learn It), your small group will be challenged to make life application together as a group (Live It). It's the way Bible study should be. Courses vary from seven to nine sessions.

- Christian Character
- Prayer
- Fruit of the Spirit
- Spiritual Disciplines
- Loving God and Others
- Spiritual Gifts

Multimedia Bible Study Kits

In conjunction with The Wilberforce forum, a division of Prison Fellowship, we are pleased to offer two dynamic studies that are at the cutting edge of culture and Christianity. Each kit contains twelve sessions and includes a leader guide, six participant guides, a CD (and transcript), and a video that includes presentations by Charles Colson and others.

- CounterCultural Christians: Exploring a Christian Worldview (12 sessions)
- Playing God?: Facing the Everyday Ethical Dilemmas of Biotechnology

111326

EVALUATION FOR

Small Group Ministry in the 21st Century

Please help Group Publishing, Inc., continue to provide innovative and useful resources for ministry. Please take a moment to fill out this evaluation and mail or fax it to us. Thanks!

Group Publishing, Inc.
Attention: Product Development
P.O. Box 481
Loveland, CO 80539
Fax: (970) 292-4370

1. As a whole, this book has been (circle one)
   not very helpful   *very helpful*
   1   2   3   4   5   6   7   8   9   10

2. The best things about this book:

3. Ways this book could be improved:

4. Things I will change because of this book:

5. Other books I'd like to see Group publish in the future:

6. Would you be interested in field-testing future Group products and giving us your feedback? If so, please fill in the information below:

Name _____

Church Name _____

Denomination _____ Church Size _____

Church Address _____

City _____ State _____ ZIP _____

Church Phone _____

E-mail _____

3 4711 00195 9412